DIGITAL ALCHEMY

Printmaking techniques for fine art, photography, and mixed media

Bonny Pierce Lhotka

New Riders | VOICES THAT MATTER™

Digital Alchemy: Printmaking techniques for fine art, photography, and mixed media
Bonny Pierce Lhotka

New Riders

1249 Eighth Street
Berkeley, CA 94710
510/524-2178
510/524-2221 (fax)

Find us on the Web at: www.newriders.com
To report errors, please send a note to errata@peachpit.com

New Riders is an imprint of Peachpit, a division of Pearson Education.

Project Editor: Nikki Echler McDonald
Development and Copy Editor: Jan Seymour
Production Editor: Hilal Sala
Indexer: Karin Arrigoni
Cover Design: Mimi Heft
Composition and Interior Design: Kim Scott, Bumpy Design
Media Producer: Eric Geoffroy

ISBN 13: 978-0-321-73299-6
ISBN 10:   0-321-73299-5

9 8 7 6 5 4 3 2 1

Printed and bound in the United States of America

This book is dedicated to my mom and dad, who are no longer here to see it reach completion. Their creativeness in finding value in junkyards, collecting useful ephemera, and frugality learned during a lifetime of running a small business have directly impacted who I am today. Thanks Mom and Dad—this one's for you.

About the Author

 Bonny Lhotka graduated from Bradley University in 1964, where she majored in painting and printmaking. In 1986, she added a Macintosh computer to her studio tools, and today continues her innovation with new approaches to her work.

Her artwork is commissioned by, or is included in, several hundred collections including Consumer Electronics Association, Lucent Technologies, United Airlines, Johnson Space Center, Vestas, Crickett, Qwest, U.S. Department of State, Charles Schwab, the City of Denver, Wells Fargo, The Boeing Company, American Society of Clinical Oncology, and a large number of private collections. Her work is shown internationally and appears in numerous books and articles featuring experimental media. She is listed in Who's Who in American Art and Who's Who of American Women.

In 1997, Bonny organized "Digital Atelier: A printmaking studio for the 21st century" at the Smithsonian American Art Museum and was an Artist-in-Residence there for 21 days. She is the recipient of the Smithsonian/Computerworld Technology in the Arts Award.

Bonny worked with a group of curators to help them envision the potential of digital printmaking in "Media for a New Millennium," a work-tank/think-shop organized by the Vinalhaven Graphic Arts Foundation. As one of three artists of the Digital Atelier, Bonny was invited by Marilyn Kushner of the Brooklyn Art Museum to show a selection of work and demonstrate how to create and combine original digital prints with traditional printmaking and photographic processes.

Over the past decade, Bonny has continued her work as an experimental artist, inventing new processes, materials and technologies, and combining them with classic fine art materials and techniques. Aside from many one-artist exhibitions, she is in demand as a speaker, educator, author, and artist. Recently, she has worked with major corporations to explore fine art applications for their products. Within this book, Bonny assembles a collection of those techniques that you can add to your own studio.

Artist Statement

Time is a fluid medium to be manipulated the same as paint. My art explores the continuum of time. I gather images by looking closely at them in an historical aspect. I look for surfaces that reflect the passage of time. Creating the equivalents in paint and pixels is a process of exploration as I allow the spontaneous layers of painting to dictate the direction of each piece. By layering images, I integrate meanings that invoke a response by the viewer. By looking at the past and responding intuitively, I explore the future by applying knowledge of the present. I use deep rich color to express my excitement over the process of creativity. I reinterpret everyday objects from the past and present to create new meaning. Some of these objects are from flea markets or the remains of my own earlier work.

Through life, I gather memories and communicate my emotional response through the use of textural surfaces, real and implied. My art is a continuum. It is a non-identical reflection of who I am. Each day adds to and changes my past. My art is who I am. Without it I would cease to exist. It is a passionate and compelling reason to live. It is the excitement of not knowing what new image will appear that takes me to the studio. Each day is a gift. I paint for myself and hope someone else gets my message. It is like sending a message to the universe hoping someone will see.

Acknowledgments

This book is the product of many years of my own research and development, but it wouldn't have happened without the additional efforts of a great team standing behind me.

I'd first like to thank my son Doug Lhotka, who took my rough thoughts and shaped them into a logical whole that I could submit to Peachpit Press. He kept me focused on organizing 20 years of experiments and inventions, and kept me from adding new ones as we were writing. He knows my work and how I think, and he has always been an honest sounding board (and great ghost writer) for my creations. Without his help, advice, and attention to detail, this book would not be in your hands.

Doug and I would both like to thank Jan Seymour, Nikki McDonald, Glenn Bisignani, Mimi Heft, Hilal Sala, Kim Scott, and the rest of the Peachpit crew. They took our manuscript and turned it into the gorgeous book you hold in your hands. Their efforts made this a wonderful creative process, and I've learned to respect their talents and advice.

The enclosed DVD was a collaboration with my son Greg Lhotka. As a sound engineer, he was invaluable in providing his editing skills for the entire suite of DVDs, which formed a foundation for this book. His passionate response to my work has been a source of joy throughout my career.

My husband Joe has been incredibly supportive over the years, and understands when the kitchen blender disappears into the studio, or the garage fills up with found treasures!

I continue to be thankful that I started experimenting with this technology in the early 1990s. Since then, many corporations have provided access to their software, hardware, printers, lasers, and materials to experiment on. I'd like to thank Adobe Systems, Hewlett-Packard, Encad, Epson, Mutoh, Roland DG Corporation, and Universal Laser Systems, among many others. Please check the book's website (www.digitalalchemybook.com) for links to the products that I've used—those companies directly supported the creation of these processes.

Since those early days, I've been blessed by my fellow founders of Digital Atelier, Dorothy Simpson Krause and Karin Schminke. From collaborating on processes, to participating in our tenure at the Smithsonian, I value their passion, minds, and friendship. Without their participation, paintable inkjet precoats would not be on the market today.

Table of Contents

Preface
The Value of Atoms *or* Print is Dead—Long Live Print

Alexis Gerard

I first came across Bonny's work in the fall of 1999 on the floor of the late lamented Seybold show—in those days *the* place to be in order to see the very latest in printing technology. Whereas a bevy of other exhibits, mostly from printer manufacturers, strove mightily to demonstrate that digital printers could at last match the quality of photographic printing (in fact they could not—yet), Bonny and her Digital Atelier colleagues Dorothy Simpson Krause and Karin Schminke were showing something completely different: stunning prints of images that appeared to extend both forward and backward from the two dimensional plane, achieved through a pioneering combination of digital printing and lenticular technology. They were, without a doubt, the highlight of the show from my standpoint.

Eleven years later, the significance of that exhibit stands out in (pardon the pun) even greater relief. The ability for digital printers to match traditional photographic output is now beyond question. The broader picture, however, is that the ability of print to simply display a two-dimensional image is, for the most part, rapidly becoming irrelevant.

Ever since the invention of paper, its purpose has been simply to display markings—text or images—better than any other physical support. Today, it is being supplanted in that basic role by billions of web-enabled displays. Their viewing quality can, for all mainstream uses, match paper. They're also capable of displaying moving images, and they are infinitely "reusable" with new content. It started, of course, with personal computers, but the real driving factor is the advent of smart phones. Just a few days ago Apple and Google announced they are each activating over 200,000 new devices *per day*. And the trend toward electronic viewing will further accelerate now that Apple has dreamed up and successfully implemented the right concept for a tablet, whose larger screen makes it much more suitable for image viewing—with competitors sure to follow.

Much as film, once the uncontested medium for recording images, is now largely relegated to one-time-use cameras, with digital cameras becoming the mainstream instrument for capturing photographs, physical printing—or hard copy, as it's called in the technology industry—is being displaced as the mainstream method of displaying images by electronic displays which show virtual—not physical—images. Physical displays where the image is not separable from its support are in effect becoming what could be called *one-time-use displays*. And that is where a stunning transformation, one that can indeed be called a *Digital Alchemy*, occurs: Far from becoming obsolete as a result of these trends, physical printing is taking on a whole new dimension of value that is based, precisely, on its physical, tangible, non-virtual nature.

To understand how and why, we need to step back and examine a key distinction the digital age has introduced in our lives: That between atoms and bits. MIT Media Lab head Nicholas Negroponte, who popularized the notion in his best-selling *Being Digital* book, cites an anecdote where, when visiting the headquarters of a large electronics corporation, he is asked by the receptionist to declare the specifics of the laptop he's carrying with him—model, serial number, and value. "'Roughly, between one and two million dollars,' I said. 'Oh, that cannot be, sir,' she replied. 'What do you mean? Let me see it.' I showed her my old PowerBook and she estimated its value at $2,000. She wrote down that amount and I was allowed to enter the premises. The point is that while the atoms were not worth that much, the bits were almost priceless."

Just as the value of information—a virtual entity—can be completely divorced from the value of the hardware that carries it, an object such as a print can acquire, by virtue of its physical medium, a value that goes far beyond that of the image it displays. The property that is rising to the fore is *object-ness*, which can confer tremendous value if cultivated with technique and artistic sensibility. Bonny's work and her teachings are once again at the leading edge of that transformation.

Eleven years after the Seybold show I mentioned in my opening sentence, Bonny's lenticular prints, which have evolved as new software techniques and hardware materials have become available, are still state of the art: they can't be matched by any electronic display commercially available today. And she has pushed into fascinating and powerful techniques that enable printing on metal, wood, linen, marble, plexiglas, and other materials, thereby creating beautiful hard-copy objects where the substrate and the process are equal partners with the image in creating value. These techniques are the universe whose door is opened by this book.

About Alexis Gerard

After holding executive positions in new technologies marketing with Apple Computer throughout the 1980s, Alexis Gerard founded imaging think-tank Future Image, Inc. in 1991. From 1997 to 1998, he also held the positions of president and executive director of the Digital Imaging Group (DIG), an industry consortium founded by Adobe, Canon, Eastman Kodak, Fuji, Hewlett-Packard, IBM, Intel, Live Picture, and Microsoft to promote the growth of digital imaging, now merged into the International Imaging Industry Association. Gerard chaired the inaugural conference of the Digital Imaging Marketing Association (1995), then launched the Mobile Imaging Executive Summit (2003), now renamed the 6Sight® Future of Imaging executive conference. He is co-author of *Going Visual: Using Images to Enhance Productivity, Decision Making and Profits* (Wiley, 2005). His opinions have been quoted at various times in the *Wall Street Journal*, *New York Times*, *Boston Globe*, *San Francisco Chronicle*, *International Herald Tribune*, *USA Today*, *Financial Times*, *Newsweek*, *Business Week*, and other leading business and technology publications.

A passionate photographer since his twenties, Gerard is a member of the International Advisory Council of the George Eastman House. His photography has been published in *JPG Magazine*, and in *Photo Op: 52 Weekly Ideas for Creative Image-Making* (Focal Press, 2010).

Foreword
Alchemy for Everyone© 2010

Dr. Carol Pulin

Bonny Lhotka's transfer prints are absolutely magnificent. That's a direct visual observation. Her subjects drawn from the natural world, from garden views to the close-up of a particular plant or the configuration of a flower, turn into richly detailed artworks of sophisticated beauty enhanced by their clear, modern presentation. Glittery postmodern architectural structures become gorgeous odes to the interplay of light. The relationship between the picture and its expression seems perfect every time. Bonny uses her response to the scene, her attention to memories that affect its emotional meaning, to determine the composition. Her excitement in developing contemporary ways to communicate that impression shows. The intellectual meaning reveals links to past and present, the progression of time, and a particular, defined location. Her combinations of traditional and experimental techniques, of illusion (the printed image) and reality (the art object), balance perfectly.

I'm a print curator. Why am I so passionate about these artworks based largely on photographic imagery? It isn't just that the images have been manipulated in ways that change the expression from capturing and reproducing a specific delimited segment of the real world into an expression of the artist's view of it as reflected in the continuum of her own life and work. For me, it's inextricably bound up with symbolic and conceptual theories about the way our minds process content, transferring spontaneous impressions onto the background of previous experiences, creating the intricately layered prints that are our memories. Similarly, Bonny's reworking of her photographic files reveals her printmaker's aesthetic—the markmaking, the quality of line, the shading and modeling, the graphic expression of values. Add the complexity of layers of translucent and opaque color to control the compositional emphasis, and you'll begin to see the reasons why I'm immediately drawn to these works, and why I come back to them again and again. But the most significant reason is how the transfer—for me, the essential quality of all printmaking—visibly alters the imagery, style, form, and meaning, the synthesis that creates a successful work of art. Bonny's creation of new transfer techniques allows the distinctive characteristics of printmaking to enrich both drawn and photographic imagery, both traditional and digital, with a wonderfully expanded range of materials, and the results really do expand the idea of print.

Computer languages evolved quickly from binary code to a graphical interface, and output from magnetic tape and punch cards to pen plotters capturing diagrams. Dot matrix, laser, and inkjet printers soon followed with color in dye and pigment inks. Jagged, pointillist blocks of color resolved into smaller and smaller pixels until the ink droplets became too fine to see. Yet artists, curators, and connoisseurs who saw the potential for computers in printmaking still complained about the sameness of the slick surface on the only useable papers. We missed the toothy textures of hand-made sheets and the swirling fibers of Oriental papers. We missed the ink standing up from the incised lines of an intaglio plate, floating over the surface from a litho, flooded through a screen, pressed deeply below the surface by a relief block. We missed the grain of the wood itself pressing its texture into the sheet; the contrast between areas flattened to silky smooth and the velvet of ink absorbed into the pricked fibers from a drypoint or mezzotint. Relatively recently, inkjet printers improved to accept somewhat thicker and rougher paper and other types of sheets. Now, Bonny shows you processes to transfer ink to a full range of papers using release films and gels, and what's more, she has also developed techniques and environmentally-safe chemistry to let printmakers transfer imagery to porous and nonporous materials of almost any shape.

No wonder artists want to know, "How did she do that?" It's alchemy, the construction of all complex entities from the simplest parts. Yes, the ancient alchemists sought to identify the most basic elements (Earth, Air, Fire, and Water) and explain their transformation into all the materials of the world. Later alchemists who tried to turn lead into gold kept their work secret, knowing that gold would still glitter but not be as valuable if easy to come by. Printmakers, on the other hand, are among the most sharing people in the world—right up there with gardeners, who readily share seeds that will magically transform into a whole world of plants. Bonny not only answers those people who ask about her techniques and materials, she actively seeks to disseminate information. She knows that no two printmakers will interpret an image in the same way, so that each person using these methods will create notably different works of art. And that's the fun part, seeing what different artists do with these media, how their personalities and styles alter their viewpoint and how they use transfer techniques to infuse those interpretations into their prints.

Some of you come to this book looking for a way to create on paper (or cloth, wood, metal, plastic, etc.) a print that actually has the characteristics you already see in your mind's eye. Other artists want the techniques to spark their imagination and inspire them to see their pictures in new ways. In either case, remember that the greatest joys in printmaking come from letting the printmaking process itself inform the work. Each method brings with it a different set of qualities, a resonance with the materials that changes the appearance of marks and lines, colors, textures, even the reflectivity of light. Each affects the additive layers differently, requires compromises that strengthen the composition or expand the options. Each offers ways to turn a straight "realistic" photograph into your own personal commentary, or change a drawing from a depiction of shapes into an exploration of the qualities of marks. The more you think of the transfer as an essential aspect of the creation of the artwork, the more you think like a printmaker, the more you'll transform the captured image into your own individual, freely translated expression of personal and universal values.

So now it's up to you as artists. To learn the craft so that you can count on these techniques in your toolbox, and in fact be ready to experiment with them to invent new methods that allow your images to appear as you imagine them. You need to consider which type of transfer will modify your initial photograph to focus attention on the reflective surface that first caught your eye, or echo the shimmer by incorporating mirror or metal. Altering a grainy texture by manipulating the resolution can play just right against a surface that is actually smoother or rougher, waxy or pitted. Or maybe it's a question of echoing the deep rich color of a backlit leaf by transferring ink to a transparent substrate, then adding softly translucent or darkly opaque layers. And then there's the whole realm of atmospheric effects on the dry, chalky surface of fresco. The combinations of printed ink and actual textures are endless, allowing the subject and object to interact in the real world.

I'm eager to see the variety of expression, the pairing of message and imagery, the synergy of ideas and materials, that each individual artist will develop using these exciting printmaking techniques.

About Dr. Carol Pulin

Dr. Pulin is director of the American Print Alliance, a consortium of non-profit printmakers' councils in the United States and Canada. She is also editor of *Contemporary Impressions*, the journal of the American Print Alliance. Dr. Pulin has previously published articles and written about Bonny Lhotka and the other artists in the Digital Atelier, Dorothy Simpson Krause and Karin Schminke; see the index for *Contemporary Impressions* at www.PrintAlliance.org.

SECTION I

BASICS

1

INTRODUCTION

Welcome! You're about to embark on a path of discovery, trial and error, mistakes, and serendipitous accidents. That's the same path that has led me to create the processes in this book, processes that let you transfer images to virtually any surface while simply using your desktop printer, and processes that let you print directly onto a whole range of custom surfaces using that same printer. I'm an experimental artist and an alternative photographer; if someone tells me that I can't do something, that it won't work, or it's crazy, then I'm likely to go try it. Along the way, I make mistakes, some to avoid and others that have become an integral part of my artwork. It is while journeying on this path that I've found I enjoy sharing these discoveries with other artists and photographers.

Throughout my career, my work has reflected a key theme: a continuum of time. I liken it to an archaeological site. No matter the media, I create a series of layers, hiding and exposing themes, color, or movement from one layer to another. The oldest image is first, followed by each younger one. Yet the final work is the product of all those layers combined. No matter if it's collograph or silkscreen prints, watercolor, oil or acrylic paintings, monographic transfers or cast paper images, the layers are still present. And now that I've added the digital tools to my palette, I create works that are either a combination of physical and digital layers, or pure digital creations. I like my creations to have physicality to them; even if it's just a photograph on glass, there's a presence to the image that you rarely find with flat media.

FIGURE 1.1 *Green Street* 36" x 36". UV-cured pigment on acrylic sheet over pearl pigment paint.

Often I find that the tools don't exist to create the result that I'm seeking, so I go make them myself. In the 1980s when I worked with cast paper, I had to design my own hydraulic press to create the paper. I still have that press and have 'recycled' it for use in my new work (though my sons no longer use it to flatten their bologna sandwiches!). What's more, this idea of melding old and new has driven me to combine photography and painting in my more recent work.

In another situation, I had the opportunity to work on the new UV flatbed printers for a year (see Chapter 23). After exploring that technology, I realized that I'd never be able to have one of these expensive printers in my own studio; I had to come back down to reality. But the experience of using them, the white inks, and custom substrates led me to find ways to get nearly the same look while using desktop inkjet printers that cost as little as $100. These alternative processes, along with many others I have developed, can now be in the hands of every artist and photographer who's seeking a new way to express their vision; I hope you have as much fun on this journey as I have had (**Figure 1.1**).

Who Is This Book For?

Was Ansel Adams a photographer or an artist? I'd argue that he was both. Yet it's not as simple as printing an image from one of his negatives—his true magic took place in the darkroom. But for some photographers, because printing their own images was cost prohibitive or they simply didn't have the space, they left the printing process to a local lab. Those labs do amazing work, yet limit the photographer's—the artist's—creative voice. Over the past ten years, all of that has changed. For the same money it would take to set up a photographic lab, you can now have some of the best digital printers on the market, and for a fraction of that amount, you can own ones that still produce amazing images.

For artists and painters, photographs have long played a key role in their work. From taking a snapshot for later use when painting a portrait or landscape, to Polaroid transfers, photography has always been a tool on the artists' palette. With the advent of digital photography, Adobe Photoshop, and Wacom tablets, artists are increasingly using those tools in their work, but may find that they miss the hands-on approach.

I like to have my cake and eat it too—this book is chock full of techniques to bring the hand back into digital art. These techniques show you how to return to creating unique originals rather than editions. The lines are blurring between creativity and technology and with the techniques in this book, you'll see that the lines are merging together, allowing us to showcase our creativity in new and exciting ways. If you're an artist who's looking to push the envelope and expand beyond canvas, acrylics, and pastels, this book is for you. Or if you're a photographer who's looking to go beyond glossy and satin as your printing choices to bring a unique, hands-on look to your work, this book is for you. And perhaps best of all, the processes in this book are designed for the artist or photographer who owns a digital printer, whether valued in the thousands of dollars or in the hundreds or less.

I've included a DVD with this book that has a selection of lessons that show you how to do several of the processes in the book. You'll learn how to do direct printing as well as transfers to custom substrates. I suggest that for those processes, you watch the video tutorials as well as read the chapters before beginning.

What You Need to Know

First, a word on what you'll already need to know before opening this book. As long as you're able to create an image (either photography or artwork) and print it on a digital printer, you have the foundation skills you'll need. If not, there are many fine books on the market about how to take, process, and print your digital images.

This book is about what you do after you know all of that. And I've organized it in such a way as to help you easily find the information you need to get started. You can move through this book in any order you like so long as you follow these three suggestions.

Section 1 contains much of the preliminary information and procedures you need to understand to move safely on to the process chapters. You should read this section first and in its entirety.

Sections 2–4 are the process chapters. You can choose any order for doing the processes within the book so long as you first read the related introduction chapter that's at each section's beginning.

And finally, read through the entire set of procedures before beginning any one process. Not only will you need to have everything ready in advance for the time-sensitive steps, but you'll also find that some of the steps assume you have items already prepared (including materials and tools).

Please refer to the book's website, www.digitalalchemybook.com, for product information, and the enclosed DVD for process information.

Image Permanence

Art media, like oil paints and lithography, have a centuries-long tradition of durability, and we have a good understanding of how to care for and restore those works. Inkjet technology is the newcomer, and the early days were not promising. Unprotected early IRIS prints would fade in a few months. Terms like "glicée" were introduced in an attempt to bring credibility to inkjet printing techniques and overcome the dislike that some artists and critics had for technology early on. I didn't let these problems deter me, and spent the first seven years of my digital exploration working at some wonderful projects using these early technologies that, had I refused them because of their shortcomings, I'd have otherwise missed. The risk was well worth it. Express yourself first; worry about the museums later (**Figure 1.2**).

How many of us have boxes of faded snapshots and negatives from the 1970s and 1980s? Did we store them in acid free sleeves in controlled environments? No, and they faded as a result. No matter how good the media, longevity is impacted by environmental factors such as light, moisture, airborne contaminants, temperature, and cleaning solutions. The original negatives from many of our great movies are stored in climate controlled underground salt mines to ensure preservation. While that's probably extreme for most of our work, there are some steps we can take to improve longevity.

FIGURE 1.2 Early IRIS prints would fade in a few months, unless they were stored properly like this one, which still looks great nearly two decades later. *Junues 22" x 30" IRIS print, 1993.*

Make sure you choose only high quality pigment inks with high longevity ratings. We'll talk more about inks in Chapters 2 and 3, but remember, brand name inks are almost always more reliable than cheap refills. You get what you pay for, so choose the best you can afford. Once you have that good foundation, continue to protect your work by placing it behind UV-protective Plexiglas, or applying a UV-protective coating. I also recommend against displaying digital work in direct sunlight (of course, since you wouldn't hang a Rembrandt in direct sunlight either, sunlight sensitivity isn't a criticism solely of digital technology). In Chapter 22, we'll talk more about postcoats that can further protect your artwork.

In the end, I guarantee my work for my lifetime, and will replace it if necessary. Eventually, it will be up to the conservators to determine how to care for works created with this new media for decades and centuries to come. As long as you've documented all the materials you used in the work, the conservators will be able to properly preserve your artwork. Public art collections often request the digital file be provided as an ultimate hedge against conservation issues, just as the Smithsonian Institution has done for my piece there. This is a new concern for artists, and you'll need to have some sort of usage rights in your contract to prevent reproductions without your permission. Of course, if you've used these alternative techniques, the digital file cannot completely reproduce your artistic vision—your hand, not the computer, creates the work.

Backups

If truth be told, I'm far more concerned about being able to read my digital image files from the 1990s than I am about being able to produce long-lived prints. I have files in formats that are no longer supported, CDs that have degraded, hard drives that have failed, and external drive formats that have been abandoned. Part of your responsibility to yourself, your sanity (when you lose a month's work), and your artistic legacy is to preserve the digital portions of your work in a recoverable format.

As image file formats change, it's important to convert them during the period when both old and new are supported. Photoshop CS5 dropped support for the

PICT format. That means you want to convert all those CS4 files to a new format before upgrading. Otherwise, you may have a collection of bits that only a very expensive data conversion service can salvage.

And so that you actually have data that you could convert into something salvageable, it's very important to place it on storage devices that haven't failed. I have a collection of SyQuest, Jaz, and Zip disks that have failed completely (I really should throw them away, but I'm still holding out hope, I guess). My earliest burned CDs are starting to fail (statistics show that they last about 10 years), and even some of my burned DVDs have had issues being read. I've had hard drives die both in my computer and just sitting on my shelf.

This means good backups are critical. I try to keep two copies of my important files on two different kinds of media. Right now I keep one set on an external USB hard drive, and another on a DVD-R. The challenge is that both can go bad just sitting on a shelf, so I need to periodically copy them to new storage. That process prevents all of these issues—bad media, discontinued hardware, and file format obsolescence. It's a good thing to do when you're procrastinating cleaning your studio.

Final Word

I'm a printmaker at heart, which means that I want to touch, feel, and hold the things I make. I still do use those big UV flatbed printers, and I work with a sign shop that will let me participate in the printing process, but that's the exception, not the rule. I keep hoping that technology's relentless pace will bring the cost of those printers down to where I can afford to have one of the big ones in my own studio (and when it does, watch for another book!). Until then, I split my studio between pushing the envelope of the future and working in the reality of today (**Figure 1.3**).

I hope as you use the methods and processes in this book (as well as those on the DVD) that you find new inspiration and your own creative voice to build upon your work.

FIGURE 1.3 From a large studio to a basement workshop, you can use this book to extend your work to whole new levels.

2

MATERIALS

You'll notice as you work through this book (and view the included DVD) that we'll be using many different materials, including surfaces onto which you'll transfer your image and the transfer mediums themselves. Each of the items you use adds something unique to your artwork. My goal for you is that in the end, you'll gain the experience to comfortably and safely go off and experiment with other products of your choice.

You'll have to collect some materials for your studio in order to try out the processes in this book. These are mostly everyday items that you're likely to have in your studio or home, or that you can find at the corner drug or hobby store. There are a few specialty items, like transfer film, that you will need to buy.

For a regularly updated product information list, check the book's website: www.digitalalchemybook.com.

Substrates

CAUTION: *I'll talk more about safety in the next chapter, but do remember one thing now: art materials and supplies need to be treated carefully— don't store your lunch and your transfer gelatin in the same refrigerator!*

The *substrate* is the surface that will receive your image, either by transferring to it or directly printing on it. In some cases, the substrate will become part of the final work, and can be a natural or synthetic material that is either rolled or rigid. There are several substrates that we'll use throughout the book.

> HINT: *Some people call it printing, while others refer to it as imaging. Either way, it's what happens when you place blank paper (or another substrate) into a printer and get a finished work out of it.*

Rigid Substrates

Many of our processes use a substrate that is rigid and can be framed or mounted without requiring the use of glass. I've made works as large as 4' by 8' using these techniques.

Dibond is one of my favorite substrates. It's a rigid composite material, with two outer thin sheets of aluminum bonded to a core. These panels have a clear finish over the color, and are available in brushed aluminum, copper, bronze, and gold. The reflective surface is an outstanding choice for the SuperSauce transfer processes in Section 2, and for the new technology processes in Chapter 23. You'll end up with a highly reflective image and crystal clear color (**Figure 2.1**).

Econolite is a similar composite panel that is less expensive and has a corrugated core. These panels have one side that is finished at the factory using a high-gloss colored polyester coating, while the back side is unpainted mill-finished aluminum. We'll actually use the back side of the panels for most of our processes in this book, but the SuperSauce transfer will also work on the white painted side (**Figure 2.2**).

The only challenge is that both Dibond and Econolite panels can be difficult to cut, but you can find pre-cut panels on the Internet, or buy them at your local sign shop and have them cut to size. Unfortunately, they're not sold in art supply stores.

I like to use natural or composite wood products as a substrate, since it gives a rich texture to the final work. Medex is a composite wood product from SierraPine. I really prefer this material over standard particle board because it has a formaldehyde-free adhesive holding it together. Dimensionally stable, it's resistant to warping and is a top choice for creating digital frescos. I route off ½" of the edge to create a visual setback for these panels (**Figure 2.3**).

Baltic birch boxes and panels are a good base for many of the processes. They're my choice for the acrylic transfer in Chapter 12. Birch is a quality hardwood with a tight, smooth grain. Because birch is not as dimensionally stable as Medex, large panels need some support or they must be built as a box. I usually make boxes with birch, as this eliminates the need for framing and is a clean, modern, look for display. You can even gallery wrap, or stretch, your image on the edges as well as the face. Baltic birch is available at your local hardwood lumber yard or woodworking store, and you can usually find a local frame shop or furniture maker who can assemble boxes for you. Small boxes may be available at your local art supply store (**Figure 2.4**).

HINT: When working with wood substrates, it's always a good idea to coat the back side with undiluted gesso or acrylic paint and let it dry before beginning. This equalizes the tension and helps prevent curling and warping.

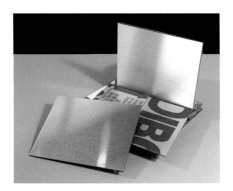

FIGURE 2.1 The Dibond panel with its reflective surface.

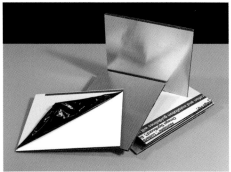

FIGURE 2.2 Both sides of the composite Econolite panels.

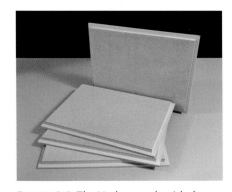

FIGURE 2.3 The Medex panels with the routed edge.

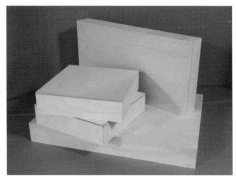

FIGURE 2.4 Baltic birch made into a variety of boxes.

FIGURE 2.5 Natural stone tiles make excellent substrates for gelatin processes.

FIGURE 2.6 Plastic scraps are a good way to get cheap substrates while you're practicing.

At the other extreme, I sometimes use scrap metal sheets or parts as unexpected substrates. With the SuperSauce transfer techniques (see Section 2), you can place images on metal boxes and even curved surfaces. Hunt online, in junkyards, or recycle centers for these treasures but thoroughly clean the metal, and take appropriate safety precautions when working with these materials.

One of the most popular processes is one that transfers your digital image to a natural travertine stone tile. These tumbled, unglazed, unpolished stone tiles are available in a wide variety of colors and sizes. To make it easier to level the tiles, look for ones with a smooth back rather than the saw blade marks (**Figure 2.5**).

If you're looking for a truly versatile substrate, however, try using plastic sheets. These come in many different materials and colors—look for brand names like Plexiglas. It's usually cheaper to buy these in full 4' x 8' sheets and have them cut to size. If you can find a local plastics company, it may even have a scrap bin where you can find cheap small panels. Plastic panels may require extra preparation depending on the process you use, so read the introduction chapter at the beginning of each section in this book before starting any projects (**Figure 2.6**).

Carrier Sheets

There may be times when you want to print on lightweight papers, metal foil, strings, or even a skin of acrylic paint. Those materials clearly won't fit through your inkjet printer, so you'll use a *carrier sheet* instead. There are three different ways to use the carrier sheet. First, you can use it as a temporary transport when you glue materials to the sheet, print on them, and then remove them from the sheet. Second, you can use it as a temporary platform to build a collage that you'll then remove and print on by itself. And third, you can use it as a permanent foundation where the carrier sheet remains part of the artwork. Most carrier sheets are made from polypropylene, polyethylene, or polycarbonate. Each of these materials has unique properties that impact how it can be used. Polypropylene and polyethylene release almost every coating that could be put on them, but coatings and materials adhere permanently to polycarbonate. As a result, you can only use a polycarbonate carrier sheet if it's going to remain a permanent part of your artwork. These sheets come in a variety of thicknesses, so be careful to choose the correct thickness. (See the section on platen gaps, which is the distance between the paper and the print head, in Chapter 3 for information on maximum thicknesses that fit in your printer.)

Polypropylene sheets come in either high or low density. I've tried using these sheets, and while they are easily available and inexpensive, I find that the drawbacks aren't worth the effort. The high-density sheets are so hard that it will cause head strikes, which is when the printer's print head hits the media, and is very bad for your equipment and your materials. The low-density sheets can be distorted or rippled, making them difficult to use. Also, these sheets are usually 0.03 inches thick, which leaves very little room to build your substrate.

To get around those limitations, I recommend using an ultra-thin (0.016 inches) carrier sheet made from polyethylene. Its thinness is a real advantage as it allows you to use it in printers with thin platen gaps, and to build up complex substrates. And polyethylene is flexible yet sound enough to avoid warping (**Figure 2.7**). Check the book's website for product information, www.digitalalchemybook.com, or the enclosed DVD for carrier sheet tips for desktop printers.

*HINT: So that the polyethylene sheet follows the paper path and moves through the printer smoothly, you'll need to determine the natural curl of the carrier sheet, and feed that through the printer. Test for the curl by holding the sheet in the center and letting it drape. There will be a slight difference between the two sides. When holding under the side that drapes the most, build your image on its outside curved surface (**Figure 2.8**).*

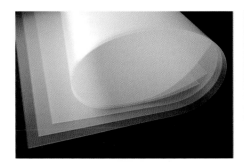

FIGURE 2.7 DASS Ultra-Thin Carrier Sheets can be used in many different printers.

FIGURE 2.8 Testing the natural curl in a carrier sheet. Your image will go on the outside curve.

ENGLISH AND METRIC UNITS

One challenge that you may have is that carrier sheets are usually specified in English units (inches), while the printer specifications are in metric units (millimeters). You can convert between the two: 1 inch is 25.4 millimeters, and 1 millimeter is 0.0394 inches. **Table 2.1** gives you some examples of various thicknesses, but *always* check with the manufacturer of your printer and your carrier sheet as specifications may change.

TABLE 2.1 Inch and Millimeter Equivalents

ENGLISH (INCHES)	METRIC (MILLIMETERS)	MEDIA THICKNESS
0.015	0.381	
0.016	0.406	Ultra-thin carrier sheet
0.031	0.787	
0.032	0.813	Most HP wide format printers
0.046	1.168	
0.047	1.200	Many Epson desktop printers
0.051	1.300	Many Epson desktop printers
0.053	1.350	U.S. dime (approximate)
0.059	1.500	Most Epson wide format printers
0.061	1.550	U.S. penny (approximate)

Precoats

A *precoat* is used to do two things. It prepares a surface to receive inkjet ink, and it prevents the ink from bleeding together or running off the surface. There are two types of inkjet precoats: those that are applied at the time the substrate is manufactured, and others that you buy and apply yourself.

Manufactured Inkjet Coatings

Aqueous inkjet printers (which are what most of us have) need to print on a surface that has been coated with an inkjet receiver in order to keep the ink from bleeding or soaking into the surface. Commercial inkjet papers have this coating already applied and can be used directly in your printer (there really is a difference between copier paper and inkjet paper!). Unfortunately, these papers are pretty boring.

Transfer film, the material to which you print your image, also has an inkjet coating on it that not only receives the ink, but also releases it when you use the proper process. This property lets you use more classic artist papers (which are rarely available with inkjet coatings) than you normally could when working with these transfer processes. Otherwise, if you simply printed directly onto the papers, you would get image distortion and bleeding across the surface. The processes I show you let you take advantage of each of the paper's natural texture and beauty. Using the transfer process with transfer film is the only way you can enjoy that highly-prized natural deckled edge that cannot be fed through an inkjet printer, or the hundreds of paper options in shades from white, tan, buff, and every color of the rainbow. All you need is to be sure the paper you choose has a relatively smooth surface (**Figure 2.9**).

FIGURE 2.9 The transfer processes let you use a range of beautiful papers.

Paintable Inkjet Coatings

CAUTION: Precoats should be completely *dry before printing on them.*

Instead of using the transfer process to move your image to your substrate, you can apply a paintable precoat directly to the substrate yourself. The precoat then helps the target surface grab hold of the ink and bond to it directly from the printer, without the need of the transfer process. There are a number of different paintable precoats on the market, each with different properties and usages. Most of these are available on the Internet or from your local art supply store. Make sure that your surfaces are grease free before applying any precoat. I recommend painting two coats on a porous surface—the first seals the surface, and the second adheres to the dry precoat and then receives the inkjet ink.

One of the oldest precoats that I've used is rabbit skin glue—in fact, I created my artwork that's at the Smithsonian using this precoat. In the dark ages of digital art (1993), there were no paintable precoats available, so the other artists of Digital Atelier and I conceived of the idea to make a paintable precoat available to artists. Most of the products available today are a direct result of our work. Until we had those products, we would wet manufactured canvas and scrape the precoat off for later reuse (you can't do this with modern materials, by the way). Things have come a long way since then (**Figure 2.10**).

Through experimentation, I've developed the DASS Universal Precoat (available in our store at www.digitalartstudioseminars.com). This paintable precoat can be used for coating custom substrates for direct imaging. It can be used on nonporous surfaces such as metal or plastic, or porous surfaces such as paper, rice paper, and gesso-primed canvas. It can also be used on a carrier sheet to make inkjet skin decals, or applied over acrylic paint to allow further printing. Each precoat has slightly different properties, which determine such things as what surfaces it will adhere to or how the ink and precoat interact to produce the final color. The Universal Precoat works for all the processes in the book. You can also use other precoats such as Golden's Digital Grounds and rabbit skin glue for some of the processes in this book. Where I have completely tested these, like with the rabbit skin glue in Chapter 20, I'll let you know. Otherwise, it's an opportunity for you to experiment.

FIGURE 2.10 *Hive*, 42" x 60", 1997. Collection of the American Art Museum, Smithsonian Institution. This piece was created with acrylic paint on spunbonded polyester fabric, coated with rabbit skin glue, and direct printed with pigment inks on a wide format printer.

Transfer Film

IMPORTANT: Make sure you reverse your image before printing on the film so it's right side up when you do the transfer. I remind you of this in each process's materials list.

Of all of the materials we'll use in this book to create stunning prints, *transfer film* is probably the most important. To complete most of the processes, you'll actually print your image onto a specially coated transfer film that releases the image during the transfer (you use a sheet of transfer film only once). There are many different films and coatings on the market, but they tend to come and go. Most of those in my first book and on my early DVDs are no longer available.

To ensure that there's a long-term supply (as well as enough for my own work), I've developed the DASS Transfer Film, available in either sheets or rolls (from our store at www.digitalartstudioseminars.com). The rolls have white tape on the edges so that they'll load properly in HP and other printers, and they work very well with the Vivera Pigment inks. Epson Ultrachrome, Durabrite, and K3 inks also work beautifully on the film, though Epson printers will need a leader or slip sheet taped to the beginning of the film for the film to load properly (**Figure 2.11**).

FIGURE 2.11 With some printers, use a white leader sheet taped to your film to help the film load properly.

With this film, your prints will come off dry to a light touch, and completely dry within a few minutes. You can transfer the prints quickly, or you can print several, and store them for many months before use. DASS Transfer Film is also relatively resistant to pizza wheel marks (left by the printer rollers as the film passes through the printer), and can be used to transfer images to other substrates using alcohol gel, DASS SuperSauce, and gelatin (see Chapter 3 for more information on pizza wheels).

There are many clear coated films on the market, available from both office and art supply stores. While some films work for some of these processes, many of their coatings will not release the ink properly, or will only release it for a short time after you print on it. Even more challenging is that the coatings may change without the packaging noting this, so you're never sure what you get. Because of these factors, the DASS film is the only one I can guarantee works with all the processes in this book. Other films may work—experiment with them to see if they'll meet your needs.

Profiles and Setup

Due to the nature of these transfer processes, it's very difficult to get an exact color match to what appears on your screen (even with a calibrated monitor). One issue is that the receiving substrates vary in color and absorbency, which impacts the final appearance. For the Epson printers, the best way I've found to get the best color match is simply by trial and error. Try using a printer profile for a heavy watercolor paper (the Enhanced Matte profile is a good starting point) and printing a few images on that paper. Then print an image on the transfer film and lay it on a sheet of the same paper. If they look nearly the same, you're good to go. If not, try another profile until you get results that you like.

COLOR MANAGEMENT

Color management is a complex topic, and beyond the scope of this book. But if you want to get reliable color reproduction, it's something you'll need to understand and work with. Here are some good books that you can use to learn more about it.

This is a good introduction to color management:

Color Management without the jargon: A simple approach for designers and photographers using the Adobe Creative Suite
http://www.peachpit.com/title/0321703138

These next two have some hands-on techniques when working with Photoshop:

Adobe Photoshop CS5 Techniques for Photographers: Learn by Video
http://www.peachpit.com/title/0321734831

Real World Adobe Photoshop CS5 for Photographers
http://www.peachpit.com/title/0321719832

And if you want a really advanced book, try this one:

Real World Color Management, 2nd Edition
http://www.peachpit.com/title/0321267222

HINT: *You can follow these techniques and get good results from many printers, as long as they use pigment inks.*

I recommend sticking with a watercolor or similar paper profile, since it uses matte-black ink, tends to keep the pizza wheels up off the print on some desktop printers, and may automatically set the platen gap to a wider setting (but don't count on that!). I prefer matte-black ink as it gives a very rich, deep black compared to photo-black. There's no technical reason not to use photo-black ink however, so you can experiment and see which you prefer. Make sure the profile you choose does not use gloss optimizer or gloss enhancer. Those coatings cause the prints to exit wet, which can increase the pizza wheel tracking problem.

If you're using an HP Z3100 or Z3200, you can use the built-in spectrophotometer in these printers to calibrate the colors printed by the printer and to create a custom color printer profile for the transfer film, rather than picking one from the built-in list. Once the film is loaded into the printer, slip a true white sheet of paper under the film and then advance the film or paper through the printer until both have emerged past the print heads (it may take you a couple of times to get this right). You can also use double-sided tape to tape a sheet to the underside of the roll of film, but I've found that to be more of a challenge. Once you have the paper loaded, you can proceed with the profiling, using the HP Matte Litho-Realistic profile as a starting point. Keep in mind that HP does not support profiling of clear media, but this technique will work pretty well. This technique will also work using a hand-held spectrophotometer (**Figure 2.12**).

When printing, set your printer at 1440 or 1200 dpi—these higher resolutions allow the ink to dry better. You can also increase the dry time in the printer driver settings on your system, but here in Colorado I've never had an issue. If you're working in a humid climate, test small prints to determine your particular settings.

HINT: *Make sure you leave at least an inch on all sides of your print so you have an edge of blank film that you can touch and use when applying the film to your substrate.*

FIGURE 2.12 If you're using an HP Z3100 or Z3200 printer, you can create a custom printer profile for the transfer film.

FIGURE 2.13 Make sure you use brand-name Purell alcohol gel.

FIGURE 2.14 A variety of additives you can use in your processes.

Transfer Mediums

You'll use three key mediums to transfer your images from the transfer film to the new surface. The first one, believe it or not, is simply alcohol gel (or hand sanitizer) and is a popular transfer medium as it's very easy to use. Make sure you buy brand-name Purell instant hand sanitizer though—it's the only one that reliably works for these processes (**Figure 2.13**).

The next medium is DASS SuperSauce Concentrate. Use this medium to transfer images to both porous and nonporous surfaces, and as a final varnish for some of the transfers. When you apply it as a primer to a nonporous surface and then reactivate it with the SuperSauce Solution, you can make transfers to metal, plastic, and glazed tile. See Chapter 4 for instructions on how to make SuperSauce Solution from the concentrate.

The last medium is commercial grade gelatin, a product that lets you transfer your image to an almost endless variety of surfaces. Details on this medium are covered extensively in Chapter 10.

Additives

For some of the processes, we'll be adding other ingredients to the transfer medium to get different effects. These may change the proportics of the mixture, so don't ever place any solution containing them into a microwave (**Figure 2.14**).

Calcium Carbonate

Calcium carbonate, also known as marble dust, is available in many different forms. The cheapest is athletic field marker, which is sold in 50 pound bags, but the color and grain may vary as there is little quality control in the product (color isn't important when you're sliding into third base). It's widely available and very cheap (**Figure 2.15**).

The best source that's higher in quality as an additive is Fredrix Powdered Marble Dust. Near neutral in pH, it's very consistent in color and grain, and is what I recommend using. It's available from most art supply outlets.

FIGURE 2.15 Athletic field marker can be used as an inexpensive source of calcium carbonate.

Hardwood Powder

This is also known as sawdust. It's often available for free from any fine wood shop. You can use it in place of or with the calcium carbonate to make a dark-chocolate colored fresco—just make sure you remove any chunks. Also, be careful to use only clean raw wood and not finished wood—the varnish comes at the end of the process, not the beginning (see *Fruit Basket* in Chapter 16). I get my supply from the vacuum bag the wood worker has on the sanding bench.

Iridescent Powders

Sparkling additives can add interest to an image and increase the apparent luminosity of the art. One of these is a quartz additive from McCloskey that reflects light beautifully. The glint of light it creates is similar to polished granite. Since it does not dissolve in any liquid, use a coarse strainer with this product as it might have problems going through fine strainers.

The other products I use a lot are powdered iridescent colors from fine art supply stores. They are made from mica, and reflect light and different colors. You can also purchase them already mixed into many brands of acrylic paint. Check the book's website for additional product information, www.digitalalchemybook.com.

It's *very* important that you wear eye protection and an appropriate respirator when working with these powders, as well as take other appropriate safety precautions. These powders tend to go everywhere, and the slightest breeze could give you an iridescent workbench (or worse, an iridescent dog)! Mica particles will float in the air and should not be inhaled.

Graphite

Powdered graphite mixes well with water or gelatin, and can add a nice color and shine to your work. It gives the look of lead, but is much safer (I never use lead in my artwork, and you shouldn't either). Since this can conduct electricity, *never* put anything containing graphite into a microwave. I use General's Powdered Graphite, available at most art supply stores.

Other Materials

To complete the processes in this book, you'll need some additional basic materials including blue painter's tape, masking tape, duct tape, tack cloth, steel wool, a hobby razor knife, a soft rubber brayer, a wire brush, and various containers, strainers, and measuring cups. You'll also need basic artist supplies like Liquitex Gesso, brushes, and acrylic paint.

For many of the substrates, you'll need to clean and prepare the surfaces. For this, I use trisodium phosphate or laundry detergent and a Mr. Clean Magic Eraser or Scotch Brite pad. Avoid using dishwasher detergent as a degreaser because it can leave a wax coating.

3

EQUIPMENT

n addition to the materials in the last chapter, you'll need some
equipment to do the processes in this book. While some processes
may require advanced printers, most can be done on a desktop
printer or with other inexpensive options like all-in-one scanner
copiers.

As we go through this chapter, you'll need to be familiar with creating
or installing printer profiles on your particular system (see Chapter 2,
"Profiles and Setup"). You'll also need the imaging software of your
choice (I recommend Adobe Lightroom and Photoshop CS5), and you'll
need to understand how to create and print images in it. I'll give you
some specific tips for these processes in this chapter and throughout the
book, but if you need more information, I'd recommend the many help-
ful guides to using Adobe Photoshop and Adobe Photoshop Lightroom
published by Peachpit Press (www.peachpit.com). I especially like Scott
Kelby's books, which are both entertaining and full of practical, hands-
on tips.

For a regularly updated product information list, check the book's
website: www.digitalalchemybook.com.

*CAUTION: Keep in mind that
equipment used for art should
not be used for food preparation or other purposes.*

Printers and Ink

The processes in this book are designed so that you can do almost all of them on your desktop printer but you can also scale up to larger formats. I use both Epson and HP printers in my own studio and have found them to be excellent machines. The key requirement is that they must use pigment (rather than dye) inks for the processes to work. Check your manual or the manufacturer's website to verify this. Make sure that you use the actual brand-name ink cartridges. I've found that replacement inks (especially the refills) may not produce reliable colors and may vary the amount of ink laid down on the media.

Desktop Printers

Many (but not all) desktop photographic printers use pigment inks, while a number of all-in-one printers use dye inks. Check you printer specifications to determine which kind you have. One all-in-one printer that does use pigment inks is the Epson NX420. This inexpensive printer uses the Durabrite inks. One cool thing about this type of printer is that you don't even need a computer—you can scan photographs and then directly print them on the transfer film (**Figure 3.1**).

> *HINT:* Most Epson printers don't support printing directly on clear media because the printer can't see the clear film. Simply use some double-stick tape (the kind that releases) to attach a white sheet of paper to the back of the film, and only put one sheet in the printer at a time (**Figure 3.2**).

FIGURE 3.1 Using an all-in-one printer lets you try these processes without needing a computer.

FIGURE 3.2 Use a slip sheet so that Epson printers will properly print on transfer film.

The Epson 3880 is an excellent mid-sized printer. This one uses Epson Ultra-Chrome K3 Ink with Vivid Magenta in 80 ml cartridges. These larger cartridges save a lot of money in ink costs, but you do have to be careful when switching between matte black and photo black ink. The printer has both, but since they share ink lines, every time you change between the two types of black ink, you'll lose some ink when the printer purges the lines of the other kind.

HINT: *Spend some time researching your printer before purchase. Some printers may be cheap to purchase, but the ink costs are high. Check the Internet for "price per page" figures on different printer models.*

Both of these desktop Epson printers, as well as many other brands and models, have *pizza*, or *star*, *wheels* in them. These are rollers that help hold down a print as it passes through the machine. Occasionally, as the paper or film media passes under the wheels, the wheels can leave dot marks, especially when using paintable precoats and some glossy media (**Figure 3.3**). To avoid this problem, you can use DASS Transfer Film (pigment inks dry faster on this film; see Chapter 2, "Transfer Film") and select a heavy media type in your print dialog box. Optionally, you can remove or raise the wheels (although this option may void your warranty), print at a higher resolution, increase ink drying time in your print driver, or try a different paintable precoat.

FIGURE 3.3 Pizza wheels may mark your prints.

The Epson 3880 has a slit on the back that you use to feed rigid custom substrates through if the substrates are 1.5 mm thick or less. Back-loading printers give you much more flexibility than ones that curl the paper when printing, and tend to have less feed problems. To use a back-loading printer, you'll need to add a platform in the back at the same height that the media feed slot is off the table (about 4" on most models). This raised platform lets you slide the flat media directly into the slot. Hand feed the media in and the printer will grab it as if you'd used the regular media tray. Epson doesn't document this trick of hand-feeding flat materials into the back slot, but it works (**Figure 3.4**).

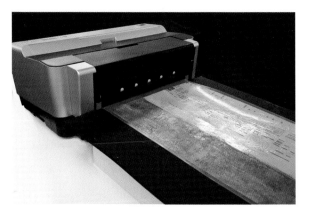

FIGURE 3.4 Hand load materials in the back slot of a printer.

FIGURE 3.5 Transfer film using an HP Z3200 printer.

FIGURE 3.6 Custom substrates using an Epson 9800 printer.

Wide Format Printers

For larger format printers, the HP Z3100 and Z3200 are great choices, and are what I use for most of my own artwork. They work well for printing on transfer film, and have outstanding print quality for photographs. For the Z3100, there is an after-manufacture replacement bar for the exit pizza wheels that keeps them off the media as it exits (contact HP for more information). The Z3200 lets you select (and you should) "Wheels up" when you make your printer profile (**Figure 3.5**).

When you build a custom substrate, collage, or paint skin, Epson 4000 or 9000 series (24" or wider) work the best. They have a vacuum platen, the plate that holds the media down and away from the print heads, with a platen gap of 1.5 mm (see below). And as a bonus they don't have the pizza wheels. A good example of one of these printers is the Epson 9800, which can print on rigid sheets (**Figure 3.6**).

Platen Gaps

The only downside to the HP Z3100 and Z3200 printers is that because they only have a 0.8mm platen gap, they aren't really suited for the usually thicker custom substrates. (A *platen gap* is the distance between the paper and the print head; with this measurement, you can determine if your media will safely pass through the printer.) If you're using a thicker substrate on a Z3200, you can use the Adjust Profile menu to increase the platen gap to maximum, but it's still only 0.8mm. The Epson 4000 and 9000 series printers will generally accept media 1.5mm thick (about the thickness of a new U.S. penny). Some of the desktop printers that print on DVDs will also handle media that thick. Most other Epson printers will accept either 1.2 or 1.3mm media (about the thickness of a U.S. dime). Be careful though because as models change, these tolerances may differ. Always check your printer specifications before using a custom substrate.

Read the manual to determine how to set the platen gap, and be very careful: many printers reset this to the default after each and every print!

> CAUTION: *Head strikes—letting the print head hit the media—are bad. If you're in doubt, don't risk your printer by using media that's too thick. I carry a digital caliper with me when I shop for new substrates and media. This can be purchased online from an industrial and scientific website. It's expensive, but cheaper than a new printer (Figure 3.7)!*

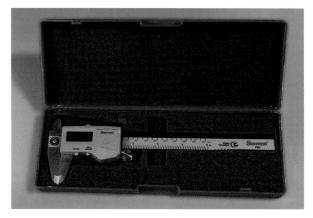

FIGURE 3.7 Caliper for measuring the thickness of a substrate.

Computers and Software

In 1980, we purchased our first computer, an Apple][+, for our sons to use for school work and hobbies. Later in 1984, I added an original Apple Macintosh to my studio. Both computers turned out to be great investments—one of my sons now works as a software architect and the other as a sound engineer! Unfortunately, those early machines, while promising, didn't have the power or software to really contribute much to my art. By the 1990s that had changed, and both the Apple Mac and Adobe Photoshop (and now Lightroom) became indispensable tools in my studio. To get started with these processes, you don't need a lot of horsepower or expensive software. However, you will need to be able to do some basic image manipulation and to print using a specific printer profile.

While this is not a book on Photoshop or on creating digital images, one key technique that you'll use throughout this book is how to digitally combine your image with a custom substrate. This gives you a good idea of what the final art will look like, without actually performing the transfer. I use Photoshop CS5 on a Mac, so your system may be slightly different.

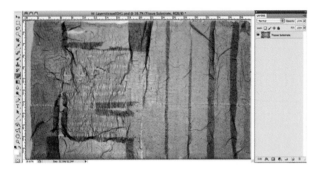

FIGURE 3.8 Open a photograph of your substrate.

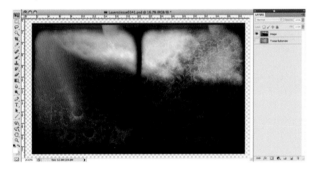

FIGURE 3.9 Paste your digital file onto a new layer.

FIGURE 3.10 Set the new layer to Multiply.

To digitally combine an image with a substrate:

1. In Photoshop, open a photograph of the substrate and place it as your bottom, or base, layer (**Figure 3.8**).

2. Open your digital image, copy it, and then paste it into a new layer in Photoshop (**Figure 3.9**).

3. In the Layers palette, select Multiply to set the new layer's mode. This will blend the two layers to give you a good idea of what the printed or transferred image will look like over the substrate. (**Figure 3.10**).

4. Using the Erase tool, remove or lighten parts of the digital file and let the base layer (the substrate) show through (**Figure 3.11**).

5. When you're satisfied with the combined image, delete the substrate layer from your file, and then save the image as a different filename. This altered file is what you'll print for use on your substrate (**Figure 3.12**). With the combined image, you'll hardly be able to tell the difference between the layers in Photoshop and the layers on the original image (**Figure 3.13**).

> *HINT: Advanced Photoshop users can also use a mask in Step 4.*
>
> *COMPUTER AND SOFTWARE RESOURCES: If you need additional help with your computer or software, again I highly recommend Scott Kelby's series of books.*

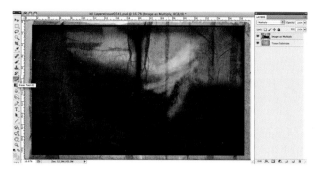

FIGURE 3.11 Erase portions of your digital file to allow the substrate to show through.

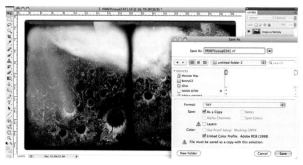

FIGURE 3.12 The image file ready to print.

FIGURE 3.13 This final work of art combining the substrate and the printed image looks very much like the layered Photoshop image did on the computer screen.

Other Equipment

There are a number of different tools that we'll need for the processes in this book. I've a strong Midwest miser streak in me, so I tend to find inexpensive alternatives whenever possible. That being said, you should never use any tools for cooking or food once they've been used for art. Every time I burn out a blender for art, I get a new one for the kitchen and use that older kitchen one in the studio. Do not mix food with art, except at your opening reception!

Hard, Smooth Work Surface

We're going to get messy. Coatings may flow off panels and onto the table (and maybe even the floor!). You'll need a large table that's completely level—use a level in all four directions and put wedges under the feet (tape them down) as needed. To catch most of the runoff, cover the table with a sheet of polypropylene plastic and tape it to the underside of the table. You can also use a large cookie tray for runoff, as long as it's non-stick. If you're not working in a studio with a concrete floor, you may even want a drop cloth underneath.

Using an Alignment Board

Nothing is more frustrating than having the perfect image and the perfect substrate, and then rolling down the transfer film and having it be misaligned. After many failed attempts to transfer the film by hand, I've developed a procedure that uses an *alignment board* to keep the film aligned with the substrate as I perform the transfer. Make sure you do this *before* you coat your substrate with your transfer medium!

To roll your film down using an alignment board:

1. If your printed film has the white edge tape, go ahead and remove it.
2. Place a panel that's the same thickness as your substrate (I'm using a second Medex panel in this example) on the work surface against the edge of your substrate. This is your alignment board.

3. Place your printed film, printed side down, on the substrate surface (**Figure 3.14**).

4. Tape one edge of the film to the alignment board using blue painter's tape. This is why we needed to leave that extra film around our printed image (**Figure 3.15**).

5. Roll the imaged film around a cardboard tube from the substrate to the alignment board. Make sure that the ink is on the outside of the tube so that when you unroll it later, the ink side makes contact with the substrate (the ink side will look dull).

6. Move the alignment board off to the side and then prepare your substrate with the transfer medium (**Figure 3.16**).

7. When you're ready to do the transfer, move the print and alignment board back up against the substrate, and then carefully unroll the print onto your transfer medium. As you roll down the film, make sure you do not let the film flop down at the end or you'll wind up with a distorted image (**Figure 3.17**).

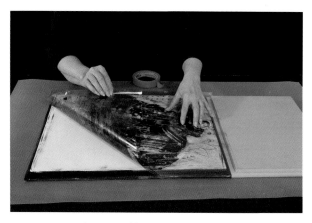

FIGURE 3.14 Align your film to your substrate.

FIGURE 3.15 Tape the printed film to the alignment board.

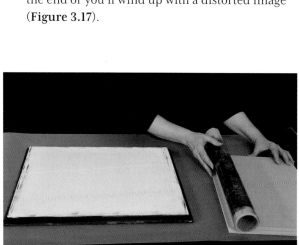

FIGURE 3.16 Roll the film around a tube and move the alignment board aside.

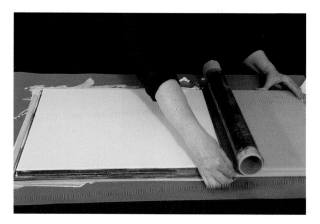

FIGURE 3.17 Move the alignment board back against the prepared substrate.

FIGURE 3.18 Roll the film down on to the substrate and press lightly.

FIGURE 3.19 Lift the film slowly off the substrate.

8. Carefully press the surface of the film down to the substrate to ensure that it's completely in contact with the transfer medium. By rolling down the film, you'll avoid having bubbles trapped between the film and the surface. Remove the tape, and push the alignment board aside (**Figure 3.18**).

9. After waiting the required time as specified in each process, pick up the far corner of the film and slowly pull the film off the substrate in the opposite direction you rolled it down, being careful to lightly press down any spots that lift up. Discard the film (**Figure 3.19**).

Coating Applicators

To spread the precoats evenly and quickly on a substrate, you need to use a coating rod, bar, or applicator. The best coating applicator is a #90 Mayer rod. This is a straight rod with a stainless steel wire wrapped around it. As the rod is pulled, the wire keeps the coating at an even thickness across the entire substrate. It's expensive, but if you plan to coat a lot of smooth paper, metal, or plastic, it's a wise investment. You can also make your own coating rod—see Chapter 17 for instructions (**Figure 3.20**).

If you're going to coat uneven surfaces or custom substrates, the DASS Coating Bar is a good alternative and is relatively inexpensive. For large projects, you can use 4" x 5" paint pads (available at your local home center). These have a fuzzy nap that spreads the coating nicely. Just make sure you wash them well to remove any loose fibers, and apply the coating in the direction of the nap to avoid any bubbles (**Figure 3.21**).

FIGURE 3.20 A Mayer rod used to apply coatings to substrates.

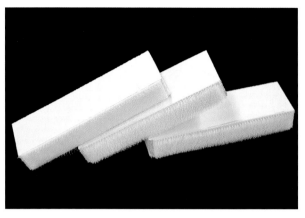

FIGURE 3.21 DASS Coating Bars are an inexpensive alternative.

FIGURE 3.22 Foam brushes can cause bubbles when applied in thick coatings.

FIGURE 3.23 Though a stiff brush can make marks, these marks can add interesting texture to your work.

Another tool artists use is a foam brush. These are a cheap alternative, but because there are air pockets in the foam, you can get bubbles trapped in thicker precoats. You'll end up applying two coats in most cases. You can also use a stiff bristle brush, but you'll get brush marks in the coating (though that may be an effect that you like!). Again, you'll need a second coat applied in the opposite direction (Figures 3.22 and 3.23).

Other Tools

CAUTION: If your thermometer has a laser pointer on it, follow all safety instructions on the tool.

You'll need all the basics, including several 1- and 2-quart Pyrex dishes for mixing and heating materials, measuring cups and spoons, and spatulas. Canning jars can also work for heating and storing the materials. Last, you'll need a polypropylene strainer for the processes in Section 3, though you can use a stainless steel one as well. I prefer polyproylene because the materials don't stick to it as easily, and it slides across the surface without making marks (**Figure 3.24**).

FIGURE 3.24 Some of the basic tools you'll need.

FIGURE 3.25 An infrared thermometer that safely and accurately measures temperatures, and a Rocket Blaster that gently pops bubbles in your transfer medium.

With many of these processes, you need to measure the temperature of certain items. While candy or probe thermometers work, I strongly recommend investing in an infrared thermometer. They are accurate, read instantly, and allow you to measure temperatures without handling the materials or containers.

Many of the coatings can have bubbles. To pop them, you'll need a Rocket Blaster or something similar. This is available from a local photo supply store and lets you have precise control over how much force you use (**Figure 3.25**).

To pop bubbles that appear between the image and the substrate during a transfer, I use a this method: While the transfer is still wet, pop the bubbles with a pin, and then wait until the surface is dry to the touch (about two hours). Cover the image with a polypropylene plastic bag, and use a foam block or your fingertips to rub the spot down to the substrate.

To heat the materials, you'll need a microwave or an electric fondue pot. If you're on a limited budget, I recommend the fondue pot since you have fine control over it and can reheat solutions that have additives (which you can't do with a microwave).

If you really get hooked on these processes, you may want a small refrigerator that can be dedicated to your artwork.

Most of these processes also involve specific times, so you'll need a timer. I recommend a basic three-minute egg timer. When I'm working on multiple pieces at once, I have a separate timer for each work. You can also use a digital kitchen timer.

Last, a product you'll occasionally need to use for some of the processes is a random orbital sander. These evenly sand a surface without leaving swirls, and really save your arms and hands.

Safety Is Your Responsibility

In the photographs in this book or in the enclosed DVD, I may remove my safety equipment to better illustrate the process. But in my own work and with all products, I always wear appropriate safety equipment and follow all the instructions on my products and tools, and so should you.

Many of the products and equipment have their own warning labels. Read and follow those warnings, instructions, and precautions. This is especially true for the disposal of products—follow the instructions on the label and all local regulations. Both the SuperSauce Solution and the alcohol gel contain alcohol and are flammable. Keep them away from heat and ignition sources (including the inside of your car on a hot day), and ensure that you have adequate ventilation.

Always wear an appropriate pair of impact resistant safety glasses or eye shields. These should wrap around your face and protect you from splashes. Wear appropriate protective gloves (probably different pairs) when working with liquids and powders or sanding materials, or when handling hot items. Use an appropriate safety mask for those processes that involve fine-powdered pigments or vapors. If a product's label tells you to use something else (hearing protection, for example), follow those safety instructions also. If you have questions about exactly what safety equipment to buy, ask at the store where it's sold.

Many processes push the envelope with the tools and materials involved. If you're not comfortable with them, then don't do that process. This is particularly true of printing on custom substrates—there are many variables to determining if a particular substrate is safe for your printer. I've had good luck with the brands and models in this book, but ultimately you must understand your own equipment and make your own decisions.

HINT: In the processes in this book, I list safety equipment under tools you'll need. Read this section to understand what is meant by safety equipment.

CAUTION: Keep art materials separate from food preparation items. Washing is not sufficient—you must have two different, well-labeled sets of containers, tools, equipment, and materials.

CAUTION: These processes are not intended for use by children. Never leave art materials where kids or pets can get to them.

ALCOHOL GEL AND SUPERSAUCE TRANSFERS

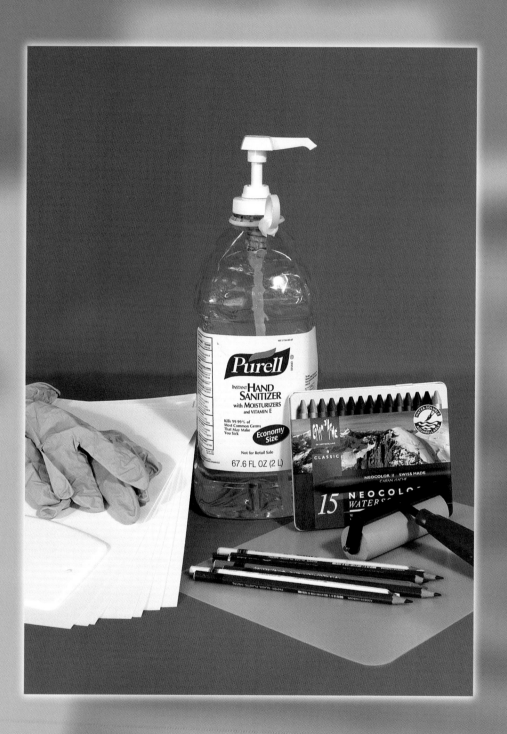

4

INTRODUCTION TO GEL AND SUPERSAUCE

Until recently, artists could use Polaroid transfers to create a unique form of art. A Polaroid transfer is created by developing the image, peeling off the backing, and then applying the image to a paper substrate—transferring the photo emulsion to the paper. The artist was then free to alter the image as desired. Unfortunately, with the demise of Polaroid film this technique is largely unavailable to most artists, so I set out to develop alternatives. The result gave me processes that keep the emulsion liquid for long enough to manipulate it, much like what was possible with the Polaroid film.

For these alternative processes, you'll use mediums containing alcohol to dissolve and encapsulate the inks as they move from the transfer film to the substrate.

One of the transfer mediums is alcohol gel, and is used as-is out of the alcohol gel container. It's ideal for use on porous waterleaf paper. With the other transfer medium, SuperSauce, you add the alcohol to it and you can then apply it to most any surface you choose.

Alcohol Gel

HINT: Stick with brand-name Purell, as I've found that generic brands may or may not work. It's not worth the risk of failed transfers and ruined substrates.

Alcohol gel is most commonly known as hand sanitizer. I was grounded once on an airplane in Chicago during a thunderstorm and was so bored I started reading the labels on the things in my purse. The ingredient list on the bottle of Purell Instant Hand Sanitizer gave me an idea that, since it contains alcohol, it might be a good solvent for inkjet inks. On arriving home, I gave it a try, and just as I surmised it worked wonderfully as a transfer medium. In Chapter 5, I'll show you this alcohol gel process. Since it's so easy, everyone who works with it likes this process, and it's a great foundation process to start down the road of alternative printing techniques.

One of this gel's properties is that if you put it on your hands, it almost immediately disappears, but if you squirt it on a nonporous surface at room temperature, it will remain there for quite some time. Therefore, make sure you always wear protective gloves when you work with it. In addition, you'll want to use a roller, old credit card, or soft scraper to spread it on your substrate—that'll further help keep it from evaporating too quickly (**Figure 4.1**).

FIGURE 4.1 Alcohol gel remains liquid on a nonporous surface.

CAUTION: Alcohol gel contains, well, alcohol. Make sure you have sufficient ventilation, and don't dry these prints in direct sunlight or under heat.

The transfer works best on waterleaf paper, like the easy-to-find Arches 88. If you dip this paper into water, it immediately absorbs the moisture and tears very easily. That's what allows the alcohol gel to soak into the paper quickly and evenly. You can also use Arches hot press paper, but it takes longer to absorb the alcohol gel. You can pre-soak several pieces and store them in a plastic bag. As long as the bag is sealed and kept in a cool area, the paper can last for weeks (**Figure 4.2**).

FIGURE 4.2 Choose a paper that quickly and evenly absorbs the alcohol gel.

Many other printmaking papers are also waterleaf, and will work as long as they are smooth to allow good contact with the film. The new eco-friendly bamboo papers from Legion Paper work very well with this process. Bamboo is a highly renewable resource, and is the fastest growing plant on earth—up to 3 to 4 feet per day. I'm starting to use this paper in my own work with great success.

SuperSauce

I originally developed DASS SuperSauce as an inexpensive way to do proofing while using flatbed printers at print shops. But it's turned out to be a great medium in many ways including creating an image that resembles a Polaroid emulsion transfer. You can use *SuperSauce* to transfer an image to nearly any flat surface that you can imagine (compared to the alcohol gel that needs an absorbent surface). SuperSauce Concentrate is sometimes used as a primer, and then activated with the SuperSauce Solution (usually on nonporous surfaces). Other times you just apply the solution directly (usually on porous surfaces). I've since discovered that SuperSauce allows you to collage images directly onto canvas, paper, metal, or even walls! It works great up to about 3' x 4' by yourself, but for anything larger you'll probably want an assistant.

Instructions for applying the SuperSauce are different for each type of substrate and are covered in Chapters 6–8. We'll use SuperSauce as a transfer medium on a variety of surfaces including metal, plastic, wood, paper, and fabric. Included on the next page is the procedure for making a solution from the concentrate. As always, be sure to read through the entire procedure before you begin. And remember to work in a well-ventilated area away from heat and any ignition source. These steps are also included on the enclosed DVD.

CAUTION: Never pour leftover SuperSauce Solution down the drain. If it picks up any water, it will form a thick glob and clog the plumbing. Instead, while working outside, pour the solution on newspaper, let it evaporate, and then place the dry newspaper in with your solid trash. Leave the solution's jar open until dry, and then put it in the trash, along with the brush. Do not attempt to wash and save the jar or the brush.

HEALING LAYER

After you've made a SuperSauce transfer to a nonporous surface and have let it dry completely, you may notice some surface imperfections. You can carefully apply another layer of SuperSauce Solution to the image using a sponge brush, which will heal and fix most minor problems. Note, however, that this is different from using the solution as a postcoat (see Chapter 22).

FIGURE 4.3 Add the concentrate to the alcohol—not the reverse!

FIGURE 4.4 A jar of SuperSauce Solution ready for use.

CAUTION: Isopropyl alcohol and SuperSauce Solution are flammable. Follow all safety instructions on the alcohol and SuperSauce Concentrate labels, and only store the products or work with them in a well-ventilated area away from heat or ignition sources. Label all your jars and keep well away from children and pets.

HINT: Never add water to the solution—otherwise the solution will turn gummy, and you'll ruin the batch.

To make SuperSauce Solution from SuperSauce Concentrate:

Make sure to wear eye protection and appropriate gloves as well as a respirator if you're sensitive to alcohol.

1. Pour a 16-ounce bottle of 91 percent (70 or 99 percent will not work) isopropyl alcohol into a dry, wide-mouth 1-quart glass canning jar.

2. Shake the SuperSauce Concentrate, and then add 4 level tablespoons to the alcohol. Do not put the concentrate in the jar first—you must *add* it to the alcohol (**Figure 4.3**).

3. As you pour the concentrate in, you'll notice that it gets lumpy and falls to the bottom of the jar. Stir the solution right away, and then tightly cap the jar.

4. Cover the jar with a disposable cloth (in case it leaks) and gently shake the solution every 30 minutes for the first four hours. If you can't do this, it will dissolve overnight on its own. When fully dissolved, the solution will appear as a thin, slightly translucent syrup (**Figure 4.4**).

5. Place the supplied SuperSauce Solution label on the jar. Keep the solution stored in the jar with the lid tightly closed to keep the alcohol from evaporating. If you place a piece of plastic wrap or sandwich bag between the lid and the jar, it will be easier to open. If it thickens over time, you can add additional alcohol and re-mix the solution.

HINT: In this section's process chapters, we'll apply the solution with a sponge brush. I recommend storing the brush in a second jar, along with enough 91 percent isopropyl alcohol to cover the brush. If you attempt to wash it in water, it'll turn gummy and ruin the brush. Make sure you label the storage jar, too!

Conclusion

As I'm writing this chapter in late 2010, I'm still investigating all the potential uses for SuperSauce. **Figure 4.5** shows the SuperSauce used over an acrylic painting lift-off technique using aluminum as the substrate. This uses a technique that isn't ready to include here, but I thought it might generate some inspiration to do your own experimenting!

FIGURE 4.5 Created using an experimental technique with SuperSauce, this 24" x 24" piece is titled *Wizard*.

5

ALCOHOL GEL TRANSFER

The alcohol gel transfer process is one of the most popular that I've created, and is a great place to start experimenting with transfer techniques. Using the alcohol gel process, you can transfer your images directly to a variety of unique and creative artistic papers by printing your image first onto a piece of film and then transferring it to your paper using an alcohol gel. The result is an image so rich in detail that it is almost lithographic in quality. While there are other methods that also allow you to transfer to paper, this process is a favorite since the ingredients are inexpensive and widely available.

It's also a great way to get started if you only have a desktop printer (rather than the larger ones available in a print shop), or you have limited skills in Photoshop. You can use a printer such as the Epson All-In-One NX420 to print on transfer film (and can even scan in your images directly first). As an alternative technique, you can cut up images to make a photo collage; the paper won't wrinkle because of the alcohol, so you can just transfer one image, wait for it to dry, and then repeat with additional images as you like.

About the Alcohol Gel Transfer Process

What I really like about this process is that it lets you get near-lithographic quality detail in your final work, while at the same time letting you add a creative touch by giving you the option to manipulate your image (like distressing the image, something you can do in the variation in the second half of this chapter). Because the inks are encapsulated in the transfer coating of the film (rather than soaking in and potentially bleeding as the inks would when directly printed onto your paper), you get a wonderfully rich appearance, very much like a Polaroid image transfer but with sharper detail and more vibrant colors.

As always, be sure you read through all of the instructions before beginning the procedures in this chapter—not only will you need to have everything ready in advance for the time-sensitive steps, but you'll also find that some of the steps assume you have items already prepared (including materials and tools) using knowledge or procedures from Chapters 2 and 3. This process is shown on the included DVD.

Remember to wear protective gloves during this process to contain some of the heat from your hands; otherwise the gel will liquefy and you'll need to start over. While not as sensitive to room temperature as the processes you'll find in Section 3, your room needs to be less than about 80–85 degrees. If you see the alcohol gel beginning to liquefy, then it's too warm (you can store the gel in a refrigerator to buy yourself a few extra degrees).

HINT: You can use any water-leaf paper for this process. This type of paper is "unsized" (which refers to a paper's fiber characteristics as it's manufactured) making it very absorbent and able to properly absorb the alcohol gel.

MATERIALS NEEDED

⚠ Digital image printed in reverse on DASS Transfer Film

⚠ Arches 88 silkscreen paper large enough for your image

⚠ Purell alcohol gel hand sanitizer (**Figure 5.1**)

⚠ Plastic wrap or cellophane

TOOLS NEEDED

⚠ Safety equipment

⚠ Hard, smooth work surface

⚠ Waterproof protective gloves

⚠ Brayer

To create an image using the alcohol gel transfer process:

1. Make sure that your digital image is trimmed to within about ¼" of the edge of the image and then set it aside for now. I like to make my images about 2" smaller than the paper so that the paper creates a visible border, but that's your choice. Just remember to take this into account as you choose your paper and image size.

2. Place your Arches 88 paper on your work surface, and then pour or squirt your alcohol gel onto the paper. Use your brayer to spread it evenly around.

3. Keep adding the gel until the paper is soaked. Next, turn it over and do the same to the other side. Make sure that you give both sides a good coating and that the paper is wet (**Figure 5.2**).

> *HINT:* Make sure that you don't have gel standing on the surface. If you do, carefully scrape it off with your gloved hand, or use your brayer to roll the excess off the surface. We want the paper wet, not goopy.

> *HINT:* You can also experiment with using less gel to obtain a faded look that closely resembles a Polaroid image transfer, rather than the rich look of an emulsion transfer.

4. You can now take your gloves off; you don't want the gel from your hands to accidentally dissolve the ink on the film.

5. We're going to use a slightly different technique to apply the film in this process (so don't follow the instructions in Chapter 3). Align your film in the center of the paper, and set one edge of the film down. Then, using your brayer, smoothly roll the film down onto the surface (**Figures 5.3** and **5.4**).

FIGURE 5.1 Use brand-name Purell—other brands may not work.

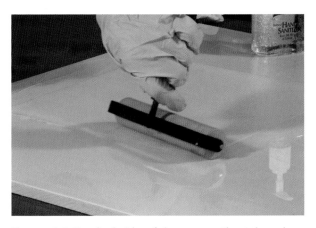

FIGURE 5.2 Coat both sides of the paper until wet through.

FIGURE 5.3 Align your film to the paper's center and then set one edge down on your wet paper.

FIGURE 5.4 Gently roll down your film onto the paper.

HINT: Don't drop the film down onto the paper all at once—otherwise you'll get air bubbles and ruin the image.

6. After you've made good contact between the film and the paper, to keep the paper clean (brayers are usually dirty) lay a piece of plastic wrap or cellophane over the paper and film. Use your brayer and roll it across the film using light pressure (just the weight of the brayer). Leave the film in contact with the paper for one minute (**Figure 5.5**).

7. Remove the cellophane, and then carefully lift one corner of the film, removing it in one continuous motion (**Figure 5.6**).

8. I leave the print on the work surface to dry naturally. Wait until it's dry, and then carefully lift the print off the board and finish it as you would any fine print.

HINT: Don't use heat, a fan, or sunlight to dry the print. All of these may cause the image to turn frosty and appear washed out.

FIGURE 5.5 Use cellophane or plastic wrap to protect your paper and film while you burnish the film to the surface.

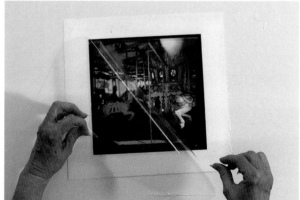

FIGURE 5.6 Remove the film from one corner in a smooth motion.

FIGURE 5.7 The title of this 12" x 12" alcohol gel transfer is *Carousel*.

VARIATION:
Distressed Alcohol Gel Transfer

Now that you know how to make a perfect alcohol gel transfer, let's try something more interesting—a transfer that's imperfect or distressed. This particular process works well with sepia toned or antique style images. The end result looks like a turn-of-the-century tintype photograph. There are a couple of optional steps in this process, where you can hand-color portions of the image. This can create the appearance of a hand-colored 1950s era black and white photograph.

MATERIALS NEEDED

▲ Digital image printed in reverse on DASS Transfer Film

▲ Stabilo pencils, Caran d'Ache Water Soluble Crayons, or watercolor pencils

▲ Purell alcohol gel hand sanitizer

▲ Arches 88 silkscreen paper large enough for your image

▲ Plastic wrap or cellophane

TOOLS NEEDED

▲ Safety equipment

▲ Hard, smooth work surface

▲ Steel wool pad, drywall sanding screen, wire, or hobby knife

▲ Waterproof protective gloves

▲ Paintbrush

▲ Brayer

To create an image using the distressed alcohol gel transfer process:

1. Make sure that your digital image is trimmed to within about 2" of the edge of the image—it's wider this time so we can alter the edge and create a more unique image.

2. Using your gloves, hold down the film (ink side up) and scratch or distress the image using the steel wool pad, drywall sanding screen, wire, or a hobby knife (or any combination of these that you'd like).

3. Optionally, use watercolor pencils or water soluble crayons to hand color sections of the image. You can use the pencil tip to abrade the ink at the same time as adding color (**Figure 5.8**).

4. Since the gel will dissolve the ink, you can dip your gloved finger into the alcohol gel and work the edges to create artistic smears and irregular edges to your image (**Figure 5.9**).

> *HINT: If you want, you can simply create a whole image from scratch by drawing on the coated side of the film—it'll transfer just like inkjet inks.*

5. Allow the image to dry completely (at least an hour).
6. Place the Arches 88 paper on your work surface, and then pour or squirt your alcohol gel onto the paper. Use your brayer to spread it evenly around.
7. Keep adding the gel until the paper is soaked. Then turn it over and do the same to the other side. Make sure that you give both sides a good coating and that the paper is wet through (**Figure 5.2**).
8. You can now take your gloves off; you don't want the gel from your hands to accidentally dissolve the ink on the film.

FIGURE 5.8 You can color your image to meet your artistic vision, as I'm doing here with a Stabilo pencil.

FIGURE 5.9 You can alter your image as you like by smearing the edges, as I've done here with a gloved finger.

FIGURE 5.10 Use your brayer to apply the film to the surface.

FIGURE 5.11 Remove the film from one corner in a smooth motion.

9. Align your film over the center of the paper, and set one edge of the film down. With your brayer, smoothly roll the film down onto the surface of the paper.

10. After you've made good contact between the film and the paper, to keep the print clean (brayers are usually dirty) lay a piece of plastic wrap or cellophane over the paper and film. Use your brayer and roll it across the film using light pressure (just the weight of the brayer). Leave the film in contact with the paper for one minute (**Figure 5.10**).

11. Remove the cellophane, and then carefully lift one corner of the film and remove it in one continuous motion (**Figure 5.11**).

> HINT: *For a different creative effect, you can press on the film, twist it, or pull the film off in an odd manner to distort the image. Remember, your photo doesn't have to have square corners!*

12. I leave the print on the work surface to dry naturally. Wait until it's dry, and then carefully lift the print off the board and finish it as you would any fine print.

Conclusion

The alcohol gel transfer process is a great process for starting out, and an excellent one since you can use your desktop printer. If you're going to try creating large images, you'll probably need an assistant to help spread the gel on the paper and roll it down. With the larger images, make sure you work in a cooler room to avoid melting the gel.

As for my workflow, I like to work on my images days in advance, distressing and coloring them, and then doing a batch of transfers at once. This means I'm doing my creative steps at a separate time as my more technical steps, which suits me better.

FIGURE 5.12 The title of this 12" x 12" distressed alcohol gel transfer is *Carousel at Night*.

FIGURE 5.13 The title of this 12" x 12" distressed alcohol gel transfer is *Bus Fair* and includes hand-colored areas.

6

SuperSauce
Transfer to
Plastic or Metal

Dass SuperSauce is unique in that you can use it to transfer images onto a variety of surfaces including nonporous surfaces like metal or plastic, and all without the use of a specialized printer. As a result, anyone can use SuperSauce. And if you think outside the box, this media opens up creative windows of opportunity.

You can stack multiple layers of transparent images to create a sense of depth, and place a final transfer on an acrylic mirror or metal layer to make the entire stack glow. Or you can simply transfer your image directly to metal to enjoy the lustrous surface it provides.

Because of the nature of this process, the emulsion is held on the surface of the nonporous substrate, and the photograph or art becomes an object separate from the substrate. This is in contrast to an image on porous paper, where the image is part of the paper itself rather than an independent layer.

In this chapter, I'll show you how to use the SuperSauce medium to transfer images to both plastic and metal.

About the SuperSauce Transfer to Plastic

This is one of the newest processes I've developed, and I'm actively using it in my own work—images directly on interesting substrates, such as plastic or metal, are in fashion at the moment. Printing on a different substrate, however, usually requires sending your image off to a print shop to have it run on an expensive UV printer. Here we'll do it my way and bypass the print shop. While this process doesn't exactly replicate those capabilities (there's no white ink, for example), it's pretty darn close at a fraction of the cost.

To transfer your image to plastic, you'll need to paint two coatings of SuperSauce Concentrate directly onto the plastic. The SuperSauce Concentrate acts as a primer, which you'll activate with a coating of SuperSauce Solution. To apply the concentrate primer to the surface, you can use a brush, a roller, or both. A roller will create a smooth surface, while the brush will provide more texture.

As always, be sure you read through all of the instructions before beginning the procedures in this chapter—not only will you need to have everything ready in advance for the time-sensitive steps, but you'll also find that some of the steps assume you have items already prepared (including materials and tools) using knowledge or procedures from Chapters 2 and 3.

HINT: When transferring to metal or plastic, high contrast images provide the best results. White or light areas in your image will allow the surface underneath to show through, either metal reflecting the light or plastic transmitting it (or showing collage materials underneath the image and substrate).

HINT: Check out the Acrylite Exotic Edge acrylics. The edges glow with either pastel or fluorescent colors and provide a nice accent to your image.

CAUTION: SuperSauce Solution and Concentrate are very sticky—always wear protective gloves when working with them.

MATERIALS NEEDED

⚠ Digital image printed in reverse on DASS Transfer Film

⚠ Clear acrylic plastic substrate

⚠ DASS SuperSauce Concentrate

⚠ DASS SuperSauce Solution

⚠ Acrylic paint (optional)

⚠ Rice paper or other collage paper (optional)

TOOLS NEEDED

⚠ Safety equipment

⚠ Hard, smooth work surface

⚠ Brushes

⚠ Blue painter's tape

⚠ Sponge roller for SuperSauce Concentrate

⚠ Sponge brush for SuperSauce Solution

⚠ Brayer

⚠ Pin

⚠ Polypropylene bag or sheet

Since we'll be using the SuperSauce Solution, it needs to be prepared at least a day in advance. It has a long shelf life so you can make some and keep it for awhile. Remember to work in a well-ventilated area when using SuperSauce as the alcohol smell can be strong. While other transfer films may work, DASS transfer film is specially formulated to work with SuperSauce. I haven't had good results with any of the others that I've tested.

To create an image using the SuperSauce transfer to plastic:

1. Prepare your digital image by printing it on transfer film. Make sure you leave enough trim to use the alignment board procedure described in Chapter 3.

2. Place your clear plastic substrate on your work surface. Brush a coating of undiluted SuperSauce Concentrate across the entire surface (**Figure 6.1**). This coating should be relatively smooth (light texture is OK, globs aren't), otherwise the image won't transfer properly. In this case, I'd like to have brush marks appear in my final transfer, so I'll use two different brushes to create a textured finish (**Figure 6.2**). The SuperSauce Concentrate will dry thinner than what you see when it's wet, but it's best to err on the thin side. You can also just use a roller for this first coat if you want an even surface.

3. Allow the first coating to dry completely, and then apply a second coating, either with a brush, or in this case, with a roller to completely coat the surface. Again make sure you don't have any globs on the surface (**Figure 6.3**).

FIGURE 6.1 Brush the SuperSauce Concentrate over the entire surface of your clear plastic substrate.

FIGURE 6.2 You can use a second brush to create additional texture.

FIGURE 6.3 You can still see the brush strokes under the second coating.

FIGURE 6.4 A frosty substrate, ready for transfer.

FIGURE 6.5 The substrate is ready for the transfer.

FIGURE 6.6 Lightly press the image down onto the surface with your hands.

4. Allow the second coating to dry completely. At this point it'll look foggy and frosty, but don't worry; it clears as we move through the process (**Figure 6.4**).

> CAUTION: *The surface in Step 4 is very fragile—avoid touching it.*

5. After the surface is totally dry, follow the steps to prepare for the transfer using the alignment board procedure described in Chapter 3. Make sure you have plenty of room between the rolled up image and the substrate—you don't want to accidently get the SuperSauce Solution on the transfer film!

6. Begin lightly painting the SuperSauce Solution onto the substrate. If your brush begins to drag, add a bit more solution to it, but don't let it puddle on the surface. Keep doing this for three minutes, at which point the primer coat should be almost transparent. Once the primer is clear and the brush slides smoothly across the whole surface, the panel is ready for the transfer (**Figure 6.5**).

7. Following the instructions in Chapter 3, roll your print down onto the substrate. Make sure you do this while the surface is still wet or you won't get a good transfer. Use your brayer to lightly press the film to the surface.

8. If you've painted the SuperSauce Concentrate on with a brush, carefully use your hand to smooth the film out to the edges to remove any air pockets underneath (**Figure 6.6**).

> CAUTION: *Avoid pressing too hard or you may smear the image. If the image doesn't transfer properly, the solution may have dried too much or been too thick.*

9. After three minutes, lift the film by one corner and peel it off the substrate (**Figure 6.7**).

10. If any bubbles appear on the surface, pop them with a pin, and then wait until the surface is dry to the touch (about two hours). Cover the image with a polypropylene plastic bag, and use a foam block or your fingertips to rub the spot down to the substrate. Set the panel aside and let it dry completely. Don't use heat or a fan—the Super-Sauce must dry slowly to allow the primer layer to completely clarify. Wait three to seven days for the image to harden before applying a postcoat as described in Chapter 22.

11. To finish the image, you can add color by hand-painting the plastic with acrylic paint (**Figures 6.8** and **6.9**), or place rice paper or collage layers behind the substrate to create depth to your final piece (**Figure 6.10**).

FIGURE 6.7 Remove the film in the opposite direction you rolled it down.

FIGURE 6.8 Apply paint to the back side of the plastic substrate.

FIGURE 6.9 Hand painted areas can simulate white ink.

FIGURE 6.10 Collage materials added behind the clear substrate can add depth.

FIGURE 6.11 The title of this 12" x 18" image transferred to plastic is *Autumn Collection*.

VARIATION:
SuperSauce Transfer to Metal

Now that you're comfortable with the transfer to plastic, let's try a different kind of substrate. For this process, we'll transfer the image to a sheet of Econolite aluminum. This is similar to the plastic transfer, and you can do it to any kind of metal, but it's important that the metal be free of grease, dirt, or fingerprints. See Chapter 2 for more information on the different types of metal panels and their characteristics.

MATERIALS NEEDED

⚠ Digital image printed in reverse on DASS Transfer Film

⚠ Metal panel substrate (Econolite is used in the example)

⚠ Original Windex or other strong degreaser cleaner

⚠ DASS SuperSauce Concentrate

⚠ DASS SuperSauce Solution

⚠ Postcoat or DASS SuperSauce Solution

TOOLS NEEDED

⚠ Safety equipment

⚠ Hard, smooth work surface

⚠ Blue painter's tape

⚠ Brushes

⚠ Lint-free cloth

⚠ Sponge roller for SuperSauce Concentrate

⚠ Sponge brush for SuperSauce Solution

⚠ Brayer or paint roller

⚠ Pin

⚠ Polypropylene bag or sheet

HINT: Check out scrap yards for interesting metal panels. They just need to be flat and smooth and completely free of grease and oil. It's a great way to find substrates at a reduced cost.

CAUTION: SuperSauce Solution and Concentrate are very sticky—always wear protective gloves when working with them.

To create an image using the SuperSauce transfer to metal:

1. Prepare your digital image by printing it on transfer film. Make sure you leave enough trim to use the alignment board procedure described in Chapter 3.

2. Completely clean your metal surface using original Windex or a good degreaser. Dry the panel with a lint-free cloth and set aside to dry completely (**Figure 6.12**).

FIGURE 6.12 Completely clean all the grease and oil off your panel.

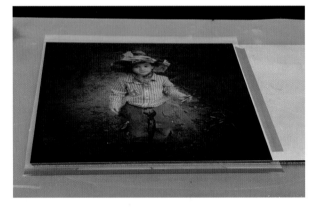

FIGURE 6.13 Use the alignment board procedure to ensure a good transfer.

3. Follow the steps to prepare for the transfer using an alignment board as described in Chapter 3. Make sure that you have plenty of room between the rolled up image and the substrate as you set the alignment to the side—you don't want to accidently splash the SuperSauce Solution on the transfer film (**Figure 6.13**)!

4. Use a sponge roller to apply two very thin coatings of SuperSauce Concentrate to the entire panel surface, allowing it to dry completely between coatings. For this transfer, you can't use a brush to apply the concentrate. Once it's dry, don't touch the surface or it will be damaged and you won't get a good transfer (**Figure 6.14**).

5. Begin lightly painting the SuperSauce Solution onto the surface. If your brush begins to drag, add a bit more solution to it, but don't let it puddle on the surface. Keep doing this for three minutes, at which point the primer coat should have become almost transparent. Once the primer is clear and the brush slides smoothly across the whole surface, the panel is ready for the transfer (**Figure 6.15**).

FIGURE 6.14 Use a sponge roller to apply the SuperSauce Concentrate evenly.

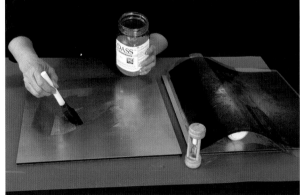

FIGURE 6.15 Apply the SuperSauce Solution and then the substrate is ready for the transfer.

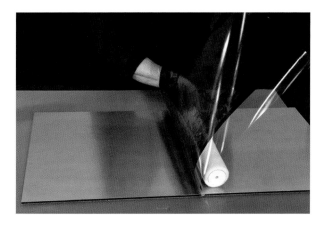

FIGURE 6.16 Roll your image down onto the metal substrate.

FIGURE 6.17 Remove the film in the opposite direction you rolled it down.

6. Following the instructions in Chapter 3, roll your print down onto the substrate. Make sure you do this while the surface is still wet, or you won't get a good transfer. Use your brayer or paint roller to lightly smooth the film to the surface (**Figure 6.16**).

7. After three minutes, lift the film by one corner and peel it off the substrate (**Figure 6.17**).

8. Set the panel aside and allow it to dry for an hour. After that time, if any bubbles appear on the surface, pop them with a pin, and then wait until the surface is dry to the touch (about two hours total). Cover the image with a polypropylene plastic bag, and use a foam block or your fingertips to rub the spot down to the substrate (**Figure 6.18**).

9. Set the panel aside and allow it to dry and cure completely, which may take several days. If you'd like a glazed appearance, you can then use the SuperSauce Solution as a postcoat, applying up to three coats and allowing the surface to dry and cure completely between each one (see Chapter 22 for more details). If you use a spray-on post-coat, allow the image to dry and cure for three to seven days before applying it.

FIGURE 6.18 Make sure you use plastic when pressing down popped bubbles.

FIGURE 6.19 My grandson is ready to ride the range in this 18" x 18" transfer to metal titled *Cowboy*.

Conclusion

Making a SuperSauce transfer to plastic or metal is one of the most exciting processes that I'm currently working with—it gives a richness to my art that I can't get any other way. Experiment with this—there are a lot of variations you can try on your own. You can layer images on top of each other using this method—just make sure you apply the layer of SuperSauce Concentrate, and then activate it for each one. You can't transfer an image directly onto a previous image though because it won't adhere properly—that's what the concentrate is for. By using layers like this, you create works that form a visual collage and have a sense of depth and complexity.

You can get different looks to your work by choosing different types of plastic sheets. A transparent or translucent sheet will allow you to place images on both sides for a layered effect. Place a mirror or metal leaf behind the sheet or backlight it to create illuminated art. You can also use exotic edge-colored plastic to create a futuristic look. Likewise, you can use other types of metal panels—copper works very well and adds a warm glow to the image. You can even bend the metal or use tubes or cylinders to create a digital sculpture. Experiment and have fun; you'll be amazed at what you can do with these materials.

7

SuperSauce Transfer to Wood

n the last chapter, I showed you how to transfer images to nonporous materials like metal and plastic. The cool thing about DASS SuperSauce is that it's so versatile—in this chapter, I'll show you how to use it to transfer an image to wood. I like to transfer my images to Baltic birch boxes that are about three inches deep. This gives me a lot of options for presentation, including assembling a large image by screwing the boxes together. So even if you only have a desktop printer, you can still make that 4' x 8' masterpiece!

This process lets you transfer images to almost any wood surface—from tabletops to doors, jewelry boxes, boat oars, or even skateboards. You just have to make sure that the wood is raw—no stain, varnish, or finish. Tight-grained hardwoods, like maple or oak, don't work as well with the base process I'll show you, but if you follow the metal process using the concentrate as a primer, you can get good results.

About the SuperSauce Transfer to Wood

As I mentioned, you can use this process to create larger works by assembling small boxes together. In this project, I'll show you how to wrap the image around the edges of a box to avoid the need for framing. If you don't have access to a box, or don't want to make one yourself, you can use a Baltic birch panel or even a birch door. I prefer wood that's free of knotholes or patches, but you may want to include those as part of the character of your work.

Unlike nonporous surfaces, you don't need to prepare porous wood with a coating of SuperSauce Concentrate. Instead, you'll take advantage of the nature of your substrate and just use the SuperSauce Solution directly. If you're using a box, you'll need to prepare your image in separate pieces for the top and each side, or cut it at the margins. In this process, I'll show you how to transfer each piece separately (**Figure 7.1**).

As always, be sure you read through all of the instructions before beginning the procedures in this chapter—not only will you need to have everything ready in advance for the time-sensitive steps, but you'll also find that some of the steps

FIGURE 7.1 An example of how to cut the pieces of film to cover each side of a box.

assume you have items already prepared (including materials and tools) using knowledge or procedures from Chapters 2 and 3.

Since we'll be using the SuperSauce Solution again, it needs to be prepared at least a day in advance. It has a long shelf life so you can make some and keep it for awhile. Work in a well-ventilated area when using SuperSauce because the alcohol smell can be strong. While other transfer films may work, DASS transfer film is specially formulated to work with SuperSauce.

MATERIALS NEEDED

⚠ Digital image printed in reverse on DASS Transfer Film

⚠ Acrylic paint

⚠ Baltic birch box (or panel) for transfer, finished and cleaned

⚠ Same size box to use as an alignment board

⚠ DASS SuperSauce Solution

⚠ Postcoat for sealing

TOOLS NEEDED

⚠ Safety equipment

⚠ Hard, smooth work surface

⚠ Brushes for paint

⚠ Blue painter's tape

⚠ Sponge brush for SuperSauce Solution

⚠ Brayer

⚠ Pin

⚠ Polypropylene bag or sheet

⚠ Tack cloth

CAUTION: SuperSauce is very sticky—always wear protective gloves when working with it.

To create an image using the SuperSauce transfer to wood:

1. Follow the instructions in Chapter 10 for preparing a Baltic birch panel to raise the grain, sand, and finish your Baltic birch box. Make sure you finish all of the sides too, and use a tack cloth to remove all of the sawdust (**Figure 7.2**).

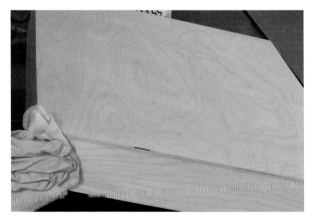

FIGURE 7.2 Sawdust will ruin the transfer, so clean the box or panel with a tack cloth.

FIGURE 7.3 Paint the box's edges to hide later imperfections.

FIGURE 7.4 Use the same alignment board procedure from Chapter 3, but with boxes instead.

FIGURE 7.5 Coat only the top part of the box right now.

2. There is a chance that some of the image may not transfer completely as you wrap it around the edges of the box. To hide these imperfections, paint the edges with acrylic paint (pick a color that is compatible with your image). You can do this after the transfer, but it works better if you do it before. Only paint the edges, not the entire panel, though you don't need to be too precise (**Figure 7.3**).

3. Prepare your digital image by printing it on transfer film. Make sure you leave enough trim to use the alignment board procedure described in Chapter 3. Cut the film into pieces for the face and each side of the box.

4. After the paint is totally dry, follow the steps to prepare for the transfer using the alignment board procedure in Chapter 3. Make sure that you have plenty of room between the rolled up image and the substrate—you don't want to accidently get the SuperSauce Solution on the transfer film (**Figure 7.4**).

5. Using your sponge brush, begin lightly painting the SuperSauce Solution onto the box or panel face (we'll do the sides later). If your brush begins to drag, add a bit more solution to it, but don't let it puddle on the surface. Keep doing this for three minutes, until the surface is evenly glossy but not tacky (**Figure 7.5**).

6. Following the instructions in Chapter 3, roll your print down onto the substrate (**Figure 7.6**). Make sure you do this while the surface is still wet or you won't get a good transfer. Use your brayer to lightly press the film to the surface (**Figure 7.7**). Run your hand over the film and press out any bumps or air bubbles.

> *HINT: Run your finger along the edge of the image, pressing down firmly. This will break the emulsion and reduce edge artifacts.*

7. After three minutes, carefully lift the film by one corner and peel it off the substrate. If any of the ink lifts off, lower the film back down and press it into the substrate with your hand. Removing it is a slow process with this material; if you go too fast you'll lift the ink off and have to start over (**Figure 7.8**).

8. If any bubbles appear on the surface, pop them with a pin, and then wait until the surface is dry to the touch (about two hours). Cover the image with a polypropylene plastic bag, and use a foam block or your fingertips to rub the deflated bubbles down to the substrate (**Figure 7.9**).

FIGURE 7.6 Roll down the print onto the box or panel.

FIGURE 7.7 Lightly smooth the film to the box while rolling your brayer.

FIGURE 7.8 Remove the film in the opposite direction you rolled it down.

FIGURE 7.9 Carefully pop any bubbles in the image and, once the surface is dry, gently press the deflated bubbles down.

FIGURE 7.10 Coat one side with the SuperSauce Solution.

FIGURE 7.11 Apply the print to the side of the box.

9. Now you'll repeat Steps 4–10 for each side of the box. Starting with one side, coat it with the SuperSauce Solution while being careful not to get it onto the panel face or other sides that have already been transferred. Apply the image to the side, wait three minutes, and then remove as above. Continue until all four sides are completed (**Figures 7.10** and **7.11**).

10. Allow the image to dry for three to seven days before sealing it with a postcoat. If you used a box, you can hang it directly on the wall (**Figure 7.12**).

Conclusion

I love the combination of the natural substrate and the three dimensionality of the box. It allows me to create works that I can present without framing, which provides a clean look (and fits with almost any décor). It saves a lot of money usually spent on framing and certainly is an unexpected presentation of a photograph. I plan ahead when selecting images for this process. White areas allow the wood substrate to show through, so I like to choose images from nature—forests or trees, rocks, or even water all work well.

FIGURE 7.12 The title of this 18" x 24" transfer to Baltic birch box is *Garden Gate*.

8

SuperSauce Transfer to Paper or Fabric

I n this chapter, I'll show you how to transfer images to both paper and mounted fabric. Transferring images to fine art paper is a lot like the monotype print process (where you would transfer your image from a plate or smooth surface to your substrate by pressing them together). This transfer process is more versatile than the alcohol gel transfer because you don't need waterleaf paper—if the paper is smooth, you can probably transfer to it. I'll show you two versions—one to a watercolor paper and another to a brand new paper made from stone!

At the other end of the spectrum, you can also use SuperSauce to transfer images to fabric that has been permanently mounted to a panel. This process is a bit more complicated, but it's a great alternative to printing on canvas that must be stretched. As a bonus, mounted fabric doesn't sag in damp climates!

On most porous surfaces, you'll use only the SuperSauce Solution to transfer your image. Painted or mounted fabric isn't really porous, however, so you'll want to use the concentrate as a primer.

About the SuperSauce Transfer to Paper

CAUTION: *SuperSauce Solution is very sticky—always wear protective gloves when working with it.*

Transferring to fine art paper using SuperSauce Solution is one of the most direct transfer processes; you apply SuperSauce directly to the film and then immediately transfer it to the substrate. In my own work, this has largely replaced the alcohol gel process because it's more versatile. For this example, I'm using 300lb Arches Bright White watercolor paper, which has two natural deckle edges and two water line edges. It's made from a very bright pulp that makes transfers to this paper show the image's colors very intensely. I also like the Revere papers made by the Magnani paper mill. The company's eco-friendly process is used to produce paper made of renewable cotton fibers in its own water turbines.

HIGH DYNAMIC RESOLUTION IMAGES

HDR images are created by mathematically combining multiple digital photographs taken at different exposures. This simulates a much larger range of exposure than you can get with a single photograph. For more information on HDR techniques, check out www.peachpit.com—there are great books and resources on the topic.

MATERIALS NEEDED

- ⚠ Digital image printed in reverse on DASS Transfer Film
- ⚠ Fine art paper
- ⚠ DASS SuperSauce Solution

TOOLS NEEDED

- ⚠ Safety equipment
- ⚠ Hard, smooth work surface
- ⚠ Blue painter's tape
- ⚠ Cotton balls (optional)
- ⚠ Wide sponge brush for SuperSauce Solution
- ⚠ Soft, clean paint roller
- ⚠ Pin
- ⚠ Polypropylene bag or sheet

I use HP Vivera Pigment inks in my DesignJet Z3200 for my images that I'll use with this transfer-to-paper technique. This ink creates an almost fluorescent glow to the prints. I also love the look that this technique gives me when I print High Dynamic Resolution (HDR) images. By using the SuperSauce to encapsulate the ink on the surface of the paper, the final work almost looks like it's been painted rather than printed.

As always, be sure you read through all of the instructions before beginning the procedures in this chapter—not only will you need to have everything ready in advance for the time-sensitive steps (especially in this case where the SuperSauce dries very quickly), but you'll also find that some of the steps assume you have items already prepared (including materials and tools) using knowledge or procedures from Chapters 2 and 3.

Since we'll be using the SuperSauce Solution again, it needs to be prepared at least a day in advance. It has a long shelf life so you can make some and keep it for awhile. As you've no doubt found out by now, you will want to work in a well-ventilated area when using SuperSauce as the alcohol smell can be strong. While other transfer films may work, DASS transfer film is specially formulated to work with SuperSauce. I haven't had good results with any of the others that I've tested.

To create an image using the SuperSauce transfer to paper:

1. Prepare your digital image by printing it on transfer film. This is where the technique to transfer the image differs for this process; you paint the SuperSauce Solution directly on the ink side of the film and then transfer it to absorbent, fine art printmaking papers.

2. Place the film ink side down on the fine art paper, and tape one edge of the film to the paper using blue painter's tape. Lift the film from your paper and fold it back onto your work surface, and then press the tape so that it lies flat (**Figures 8.1** and **8.2**).

FIGURE 8.1 Tape the film ink-side down to the paper.

FIGURE 8.2 After folding the image back, press the tape down so that it's flat.

SOFTER EDGES

I like to have a softer edge on my transfers, so before beginning I wet a paper towel or cotton ball with water to wipe the border of the image, which removes some ink and the coating from the transfer film. This is your chance to tickle the edge to make it look like an old piece of film or look soft like an irregular Polaroid edge. Make sure you also wipe the inkjet coating from the unprinted border as well, so that the image releases properly. Allow the print to dry completely before continuing (**Figure 8.3**).

FIGURE 8.3 You can wipe the edge to create a softer transition.

3. Use a wide sponge brush to spread SuperSauce Solution directly on the ink side of the film. You need to work quickly, just floating the solution on the surface. You're not trying to brush the solution into the ink, just lightly across the surface (**Figure 8.4**).

   HINT: Floating the solution on the surface may take practice, so work on small images first.

4. Use a soft paint roller to roll the film down onto the paper (make sure you don't let it flop down on the paper). The SuperSauce Solution will immediately be drawn into the paper and transfer the image, so you can't move the film around at all (**Figure 8.5**).

5. Use the soft roller to push the last bit of film down, and then lightly rub it across the surface so that there is good contact. Be careful you don't press so hard that you move the ink (**Figure 8.6**).

6. After three minutes, remove the blue painter's tape, and then carefully peel back one corner of the film. Slowly remove the film from the print. If any bubbles appear on the surface, pop them with a pin, and then wait until the surface is dry to the touch (about two hours). Cover the image with a polypropylene plastic bag, and use a foam block or your fingertips to rub the spot down to the substrate (**Figure 8.7**).

FIGURE 8.4 Lightly float the SuperSauce Solution across the film.

FIGURE 8.5 Roll the film down onto the paper in a smooth, even motion.

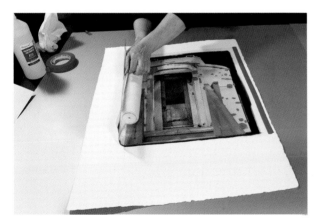

FIGURE 8.6 Lightly smooth the film down onto the paper using the paint roller.

FIGURE 8.7 Slowly remove the film from the print.

FIGURE 8.8 The title of this 21" x 21" transfer to paper is *Red Caboose*.

StoneAge Emulsion Transfer to Paper

Stone paper is a new and unique material made from crushed stone, which provides a really exciting surface for creative transfers. I've worked directly with the manufacturer to get this product available for this process. The stone paper is waterproof, which keeps the SuperSauce Solution fluid so that the emulsion and inks form a floating film on the surface as it dries. This allows us to manipulate the image to create new, artistic forms. In this variation, we'll have a chance to do this manipulation as the film is being removed from the paper. You can buy this cool substrate at www.digitalartstudioseminars.com.

For this StoneAge emulsion transfer process to work, you'll need to use a slightly different formula of SuperSauce Solution. Make a batch following the instructions in Chapter 4, but add a total of 18 ounces of alcohol to the 4 tablespoons of the concentrate. Label it clearly as "StoneAge SuperSauce Solution" because it may be too thin to use efficiently for the other processes.

MATERIALS NEEDED

⚠ Digital image printed in reverse on DASS Transfer Film

⚠ Stone paper

⚠ DASS StoneAge SuperSauce Solution

TOOLS NEEDED

⚠ Safety equipment

⚠ Hard, smooth work surface

⚠ Pencil

⚠ Coating bar (optional)

⚠ Wide sponge brush for the SuperSauce Solution

⚠ Soft, clean paint roller

⚠ Brayer

⚠ Pin

⚠ Polypropylene bag or sheet

CAUTION: SuperSauce Solution is very sticky—always wear protective gloves when working with it.

FIGURE 8.9 Mark where you want your image to sit on the paper.

FIGURE 8.10 You can alter the edge using a wet coating bar.

FIGURE 8.11 Lightly float the StoneAge SuperSauce Solution across the film.

To create an image using the SuperSauce transfer to stone paper:

1. Prepare your digital image by printing it on transfer film. With this paper, I like to have a large border, so I size my images about three inches smaller on each side. As a bonus, if I haven't laid the image down perfectly square, I'll have room to trim the final image before mounting.

2. With this process, you'll use a different technique to transfer the image, which will let you manipulate the image as it's being pulled from the substrate. Instead of taping the image to a side of the paper, position the film ink side down on the paper and make a light pencil marking where each corner will be (**Figure 8.9**).

   > **HINT:** Like the cotton ball and water method to create a soft edge, another optional way to create a more interesting edge is to dip a coating bar in water and tickle the edge of the ink. Just make sure you wipe the inkjet coating from the unprinted border as well. Allow the print to dry completely before continuing (*Figure 8.10*).

3. Flip the film back over and place it ink side up on the paper. Use a wide sponge brush to spread the StoneAge SuperSauce Solution directly onto the ink side of the film (it's OK if you get a little on the paper, but try to stay on the film). You need to work quickly, just floating the solution on the surface. You're not trying to brush the solution into the ink, but just lightly across the surface (**Figure 8.11**).

4. Use two hands to pick up the coated film, flip it over, and lay one edge down, floating the film down and lightly rolling it across the paper. Align the edge with the marks you made earlier (**Figure 8.12**). Don't press the image down just yet.

> *CAUTION:* Once it's down, don't move the image or you'll smear the transfer, and we're not ready to do that quite yet. But in a few minutes, we'll intentionally move the image for the effect it will give us!!

> *HINT:* If you're working on very large transfers, you can apply the solution directly to the stone paper. To avoid forcing the SuperSauce Solution off one end of the paper, hold both ends of your film, and let it drape to form a large U. Set the center of the film down in the middle of the coated stone paper, then gently lay down both sides at the same time.

5. Use the soft paint roller to push the last bit of film down, and then lightly rub it across the surface so that there is good contact and to remove any air pockets under the film. Be careful you don't press so hard that you move the ink yet (**Figure 8.13**).

6. After three minutes, pick up two corners of the film, lifting, lowering, sliding, and twisting it as you remove it. This forms creases, breaks, and folds in the emulsion, and creates a really cool surface. If you don't see a lot of movement, you may not have used enough solution. After you create a dozen or so of these, you will find the technique that gives the results you like best—there are no rules (**Figure 8.14**).

FIGURE 8.12 Lay the print, ink-side down, onto the paper.

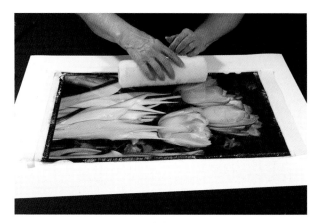

FIGURE 8.13 Lightly smooth the film down onto the paper.

FIGURE 8.14 Twist and move the film as you lift it.

FIGURE 8.15 Lift the paper to create folds in the emulsion.

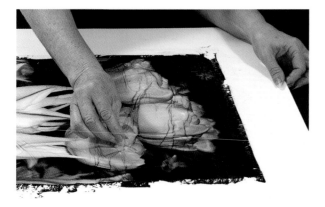

FIGURE 8.16 Pop the bubbles with a pin and then later press them down.

*HINT: You can also pick up the stone paper after you've peeled the film off, and, since the emulsion is still wet, let the emulsion slide down to form folds in the final image (**Figure 8.15**).*

7. If any bubbles appear on the surface, pop them with a pin, and then wait until the surface is dry to the touch, or about two hours. Cover the image with a polypropylene plastic bag, and run your brayer over it to flatten the emulsion to the paper. If you have access to a laminator or etching press, you can use that to do the same thing (**Figure 8.16**).

TIP: As you roll the film down onto your paper, air bubbles can get trapped between the film and the paper. Then, when you pull the film away, the bubbles form between the skin and the stone paper. I've found a way to avoid these bubbles—you create a double wet layer that doesn't trap air bubbles. Apply a coating of the SuperSauce Solution to the stone paper. Then, before that coating dries, apply a smooth coating of the solution to the ink side of the film. Use the same technique to roll the film down as shown in Step 4 above. If you prefer a less glossy surface, apply a total of three coatings of the solution to the image area—just be sure to allow each varnish layer to dry for a day between coatings. As you gain practice with this transfer process, eventually you can skip this double wet layer tip.

FIGURE 8.17 The title of this 13" x 20" transfer to stone paper is *Garden Light*.

ADVANCED VARIATION:
SuperSauce Transfer to Fabric

For an advanced process, I'll show you how to transfer an image to fabric. I love the look of linen, but finding linen already prepared with an inkjet coating is almost impossible, so it's been difficult to use this wonderful surface as a substrate. As a solution to this dilemma, I tried mounting the linen fabric to a rigid substrate, and then used SuperSauce Solution to transfer the image to the fabric after priming it with the concentrate. It works beautifully, as you'll see in this process.

CAUTION: SuperSauce Solution is very sticky—always wear protective gloves when working with it.

MATERIALS NEEDED

⚠ Digital image printed in reverse on DASS Transfer Film

⚠ Econolite panel

⚠ Liquitex Gesso

⚠ Smooth or fine-weave linen (see the sidebar "Alternative Fabrics" below)

⚠ DASS SuperSauce Concentrate

⚠ DASS SuperSauce Solution

TOOLS NEEDED

⚠ Safety equipment

⚠ Hard, smooth work surface

⚠ Blue painter's tape

⚠ Sponge roller for gesso

⚠ Plastic scraper

⚠ Sandpaper

⚠ Razor

⚠ Cotton balls

⚠ Wide sponge brush for SuperSauce Solution

⚠ Soft, clean paint roller

⚠ Pin

⚠ Polypropylene bag or sheet

To create an image using the SuperSauce transfer to linen:

1. Prepare your digital image by printing it on transfer film.

2. Prepare your panel as described in Chapter 10. Make sure it's clean and dry before proceeding (**Figure 8.18**).

3. Use a sponge roller to apply a heavy coating of gesso to the panel (**Figure 8.19**).

4. While the base coat is still wet, roll the linen onto the panel (**Figure 8.20**); for alternative fabrics, see the sidebar "Alternative Fabrics" on the next page.

5. Immediately apply gesso to the surface. You want to roll it down until the fabric is soaked and glued down completely. Then use a scraper to smooth the gesso into the fibers and remove any excess from the surface. You should be able to see the weave but no brush strokes on the surface (**Figure 8.21**).

FIGURE 8.18 Prepare the panel by sanding the surface.

FIGURE 8.19 Make sure the coating of gesso is even.

FIGURE 8.20 Roll the linen onto the panel.

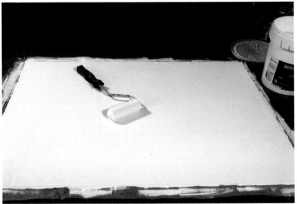

FIGURE 8.21 A fabric linen panel coated with gesso.

FIGURE 8.22 Trim the fabric cleanly to the panel's edge.

FIGURE 8.23 Wipe the edges to create a natural transition rather than a sharp one.

6. Allow the panel to dry overnight—it's better to be more dry than less. If you used linen as opposed to the tarlatan alternative, you may need to sand off any bumps in the fabric so that the surface is smooth; otherwise you won't get a clean transfer. Then use a razor to neatly trim off the excess fabric from the panel edge (**Figure 8.22**).

> *HINT: You can paint the linen on top of the dry gesso to create a more interesting substrate. In this example, I applied two coats of pearl pearlescent acrylic paint on top of the gesso. Just make sure it's completely dry before proceeding. I find that using this paint underneath a black and white photograph creates a dynamic, rich image.*

7. While your panel is drying, place your imaged transfer film ink-side up on another work surface. Wet a cotton ball with water and wipe off the ink at the edges of the image to create a natural transition (see the sidebar "Softer Edges" at the beginning of this chapter and **Figure 8.23**). Use a different cotton ball to wipe off the inkjet coating on the unprinted edge also. Let it dry completely (overnight with the panel is a good idea).

ALTERNATIVE FABRICS

Tarlatan is a less expensive alternative to linen, made from cotton rather than flax. It's used to wipe etching plates, and has an irregular open weave that looks like linen or cheesecloth when mounted. Unlike linen, it's woven from threads that are all the same size and thickness, which makes it a bit easier to work with when you're starting out. You could also use a smooth fabric with a pre-printed pattern, or even silk.

8. Place your panel on your work surface. Roll a coating of undiluted SuperSauce Concentrate across the entire surface.

9. Allow the first coating to dry completely, and then apply a second coating, either with a brush, or in this case, with a roller to completely coat the surface.

10. Allow the second coating to dry completely.

> *HINT: I make a lot of these panels in advance so that I can do a batch of transfers all at once.*

11. After the surface is totally dry, follow the steps to prepare for the transfer using the alignment board procedure as described in Chapter 3. Make sure that you have plenty of room between the rolled up image and the substrate—you don't want to accidently get the SuperSauce Solution on the transfer film!

12. Begin lightly painting the SuperSauce Solution onto the surface. If your brush begins to drag, add a bit more solution to it, but don't let it puddle on the surface. Keep doing this for three minutes, at which point the primer coat should have become almost transparent. Once the primer is clear and the brush slides smoothly across the whole surface, the panel is activated and ready for the transfer (**Figure 8.24**).

13. Following the instructions in Chapter 3, roll your print down onto the substrate. Make sure you do this while the surface of your substrate is still wet or you won't get a good transfer. Then use your soft paint roller to lightly press the film to the surface (**Figures 8.25** and **8.26**).

FIGURE 8.24 The primer coating of SuperSauce Solution is activated once the brush glides smoothly.

FIGURE 8.25 Roll your image down onto the surface.

FIGURE 8.26 Gently smooth the film to the surface.

14. After three minutes, lift the film by one corner and gently peel it off the substrate (**Figure 8.27**).

15. If any bubbles appear on the surface, pop them with a pin, and then wait until the surface is dry to the touch (about two hours). Cover the image with a polypropylene plastic bag, and use a foam block or your fingertips to rub the spot down to the substrate.

16. Set the panel aside and let it dry completely. To finish it, you can apply a postcoat of SuperSauce Solution.

FIGURE 8.27 Remove the film in the opposite direction you rolled it down.

Conclusion

Of all the processes I have developed, these are the ones that make me feel most like I'm back doing classic monoprints. By moving the ink from the film to another surface, you have the ability to manipulate and alter the image during the transfer—a more hands-on process than directly printing on inkjet paper.

Best of all, these processes bring the entire rich portfolio of fine art papers into the digital age. If you tried to print directly on them, the image would bleed and run. Being able to use traditional printmaking papers is almost like coming home again!

FIGURE 8.28 The title of this 24" x 32" transfer to fabric is *Bench*.

9

GALLERY OF WORK:
ALCOHOL GEL
AND SUPERSAUCE
TRANSFERS

Moon Light

24" x 24". SuperSauce Transfer to Metal. A scrap copper clad panel brings out the richness of this infrared photograph. I cleaned off parts of the oxidation to create a pattern of light and dark areas on the substrate. I mounted the sheet on a three-inch deep Baltic birch box to complete the substantial presence of the final work.

Rabbit Cave

22" x 30". SuperSauce Transfer to Paper. I painted SuperSauce Solution directly on the film inside the image border, and then transferred it to Rives BFK printmaking paper. This left an irregular outline that emphasizes the petroglyph style of image I was trying to create. The photograph is a combination of an old painter's drop cloth and a puppet.

Pot Pile

24" x 32". SuperSauce Transfer to Linen. I thought that it was very natural to combine a photograph of garden pots with a linen substrate. Because the fabric can be displayed without glass, the tactile nature of the work really comes through.

Blue Tuesday

22" x 32". SuperSauce Transfer to Paper. I did the same process as for Rabbit Cave, but transferred it to Arches Bright White watercolor paper instead. I started with a photograph of flowers and then aggressively altered and stylized it in Photoshop. I like the colors in my photographs to resemble the acrylic paints I'd used for so many years, so that when an image is transferred to printmaking papers it looks like hand-painted artwork.

Dump Truck

22" x 30". SuperSauce Transfer to Paper. For this transfer, I wiped the edge of the film with a wet brush to create the soft image border, and then transferred it to T.H. Saunders watercolor paper. I created the stippled grainy look in Photoshop on purpose—it's not a problem with a poor transfer!

Carnation Bowl

22" x 22". SuperSauce Transfer to Paper. I started with a piece of Arches Bright White watercolor paper, scored it against a straight edge, and then tore it by hand to create the deckled edge. I printed the image on DASS Transfer Film using my HP Z3200 and Vivera Pigment inks to get a color intensity that I cannot achieve when I use traditional paints.

Garden Kale

24" x 24". SuperSauce Transfer to Wood. My Baltic birch panel was a perfect match for this image of a kale plant, and added real texture to the final work. I started with the photograph in black and white, and added a screen filter and then colorized it in Photoshop. When I dramatically pushed the contrast, portions of the image became white, which made them print clear and allowed the wood grain to fill in the highlights.

At the Gardens

16" x 20". StoneAge Emulsion Transfer to Stone Paper. I like using infrared black and white photographs for this process, because the folds I create in the light areas become visible and give a fluid appearance to the image. Using a paint pad, I modified the edges of the ink on the film to create an interesting look.

Rainbow

16" x 20". StoneAge Emulsion Transfer to Stone Paper. I think this process matches well with the image of the fish scales. In this case, I didn't wipe the border of the image before the transfer, so I could get more movement of the emulsion around the border.

Closet Art

26" x 48". SuperSauce Transfer to Metal. This is another copper-clad sheet that I salvaged from a company I found on the Internet. When it arrived, it had a beautiful blue green patina that made a vignette around the sheet. For this gorgeous substrate, I created a custom image so that it would show through in the final piece. When I work on copper, I usually increase the contrast and saturate the colors by 12 percent in Photoshop, which allows more of the rich substrate to show through.

SECTION III

GELATIN TRANSFERS

113

10

INTRODUCTION TO GELATIN TRANSFERS

grew up near Chicago where my parents operated Bud's Steak House. I still remember my parents using a gelatin slab to print menus for their restaurant. They used a colored pencil to create an original image, and then transferred it to the gelatin. I would watch as each sheet of paper was placed on the slab, and was amazed when the writing moved to the paper. I still feel that magic every time I transfer a print using gelatin, creating a slightly altered image on the new surface. When I do this by hand, there's something personal and unique—something human—returned to a sterile, technical process.

In this section, I'll show you how to use the gelatin transfer process to move an image printed on digital transfer film to a different surface. This process works on many kinds of surfaces such as watercolor paper, travertine tile, or a marble fresco coating on a wooden board. By adding the right adhesive to gelatin, an image will stick to most surfaces, including collages, acrylic paint, wood, clear polycarbonate or Plexiglas, tile, and metal.

While other transfer films may work, I've had inconsistent results. The DASS film I developed always works for these processes, so that's what I show in each materials list.

About Gelatin

One of the challenges to creating a good gelatin transfer medium is getting the mixture's pH level just right. If the pH is off, your other ingredients might precipitate out of the mixture rather than stay in suspension. There's really no way to easily alter the pH of your mixture, so I try to keep things as consistent as possible. That's why we'll use a high-grade gelatin, distilled water, and consistent products. All of my testing has been with Golden products, so other brands may have different pH values and may not work properly.

Gelatin comes in two forms: food grade and commercial grade. Food grade gelatins are usually made from animal hides, are amber in color, and tend to vary quite a bit in both pH and bloom. Different manufacturers' gelatins have different properties, and those can even change from batch to batch. While it's possible to get good results from food grade gelatins, it's rather unpredictable.

Commercial gelatins are generally made from either animal hides or bones (ossein), and are more consistent in pH and bloom. Ossein high-bloom gelatins are most compatible with the adhesive additives used for these processes and create a nice, firm medium for transfers. Commercial gelatins made from pork will dry clear and are ideal for creating multiple layers on top of your substrate. When you want your substrate to show through, use a clear gelatin for the best results (**Figure 10.1**).

> **WHAT IS BLOOM?**
>
> Bloom is how firm gelatin is after it has set. A low bloom gelatin will be soft and mushy and unsuited for transfers, while a high bloom gelatin is very firm and ideal for transfers.

As a result, I recommend using either commercial ossein or water clear pork gelatins for the most consistent results, depending on which process you're using. You *can* succeed with food grade gelatin, but you may need to experiment a bit with different brands to find one that works for you. Just make sure you're using pure gelatin, and not one with added coloring or sweeteners. For a few of the processes in this book, we'll use rabbit skin glue granules in the place of gelatin. Rabbit skin glue granules take twice as long as gelatin to swell, but otherwise work the same as high grade commercial gelatin. I use this when I'm adding wood powder to a mixture, since it's a very good wood glue.

FIGURE 10.1 Food grade gelatin is shown on the left; commercial grade pork gelatin is shown on the right.

UNDERSTANDING PH VALUES

pH is a way chemists measure the acidity or alkalinity of a material. Values run from 0 to 14, with 7 considered neutral. Here are some example values:

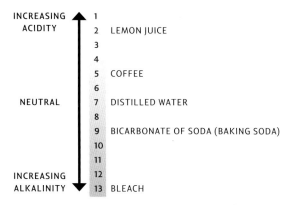

INCREASING ACIDITY	1	
	2	LEMON JUICE
	3	
	4	
	5	COFFEE
	6	
NEUTRAL	7	DISTILLED WATER
	8	
	9	BICARBONATE OF SODA (BAKING SODA)
	10	
	11	
INCREASING ALKALINITY	12	
	13	BLEACH

Water can vary depending on what minerals are dissolved in it, so it may be slightly basic (alkaline) or slightly acidic, or even different from day to day. That's why we use distilled (not artesian or reverse osmosis) water for our mixtures.

For each square foot that you want to transfer, you'll need ½ cup of distilled water and 1 tablespoon of gelatin. It's important to use distilled water to achieve consistent results.

If you're working in a warm studio, the gelatin may not set up properly (it has to drop to around 65 degrees). You can try working on the floor—it's often several degrees cooler down there—or place your panels in a refrigerator (used only for art, of course) to accelerate the process. High humidity can also impact the gelling process. Also, be sure to use the correct measurements.

Gelatin will spoil in a few days, even if it's kept refrigerated. After my studio assistant complained about having to throw out rotting gelatin, I researched preserva-tives and found that the only one in wide use is formaldehyde. Needless to say, I

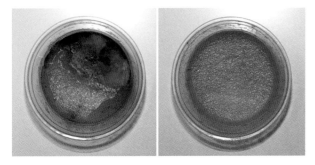

FIGURE 10.2 The gelatin on the left is spoiled; the gelatin on the right was treated with oil of cloves, which can keep gelatin fresh for more than four months.

FIGURE 10.3 If you prepare your gelatin mixture in advance, store it in the refrigerator and cut off just the amount you need for each project.

didn't want that in my studio. After reading that oil of cloves was used to preserve egg tempera paints, I gave it a try and, to my delight, it worked! So you can extend your gelatin's life by adding a few drops of oil of cloves before refrigerating it. In **Figure 10.2**, the gelatin on the left was left at room temperature for a short time without any oil of cloves. The gelatin on the right was treated with oil of cloves and kept at room temperature for more than four months. Unless you add the oil of cloves, gelatin mixtures should be used the day that they are made. Occasionally, if I'm producing a whole edition, I'll prepare a larger quantity of the basic mixture in advance and store it in the refrigerator. That's good for about three days. You can then cut off the amount you need and rewarm it in a fondue pot. The gelatin shown here is white because it contains the polymer medium. It should not be rewarmed in a microwave (**Figure 10.3**).

CAUTION: Oil of cloves is not food. Read the label and follow all instructions! It should only be used in gelatin stored in a container that's clearly marked as inedible.

Preparing Gelatin

Some processes require slightly more or less gelatin in the mixture, so always be careful to read those materials lists. If your panel is one square foot, use a single batch of gelatin. If your panel is larger, use 1½ batches per square foot (including the first one). This is true for all of the different layers and batches in this section. Larger panels take more gelatin to get an appropriate coat, but we won't want to waste it on these smaller sample projects.

Since the gelatin is moist, it's important to allow your prints to dry for at least four hours before attempting the transfer.

MATERIALS NEEDED

⚠ ½ cup cold distilled water

⚠ 1 tablespoon gelatin

TOOLS NEEDED

⚠ Protective gloves

⚠ Eye protection

⚠ Microwave-proof glass container

⚠ Thermometer

FIGURE 10.4 The tools and materials you'll need to prepare a gelatin transfer mix.

HINT: While you can get away with less gelatin than the amount listed in the materials list (2½ teaspoons, or a single packet), you may end up with a less firm gelatin coating.

CAUTION: Keep children and pets away from your gelatin panels. None of this gelatin is edible, especially after you've transferred the image to the surface.

To prepare a batch of gelatin:

Mixing the gelatin is a pretty simple process as long as you follow some basic rules. Rule number 1: Always use cold water or you'll end up with a gummy mess that has to be thrown away.

1. Add ½ cup cold—*not refrigerated*—distilled water into a glass container.

FIGURE 10.5 When mixing gelatin, be sure to use cold, *not refrigerated*, water.

FIGURE 10.6 Check the temperature of your gelatin to make sure it doesn't get too hot.

2. To the water, add 1 tablespoon gelatin (**Figure 10.5**).

   If you're using packages, each one contains only about 2½ teaspoons (there are three teaspoons to a tablespoon), so you'll be a bit short.

3. Wait a few minutes until the mixture begins to look like thin applesauce.

4. Place the container holding the gelatin in the microwave (used only for art) and heat it to between 130 and 140 degrees to activate the gelatin (which happens at around 125 or 130 degrees). As you heat the gelatin, watch that it doesn't get too hot (over 140 degrees); otherwise it will break down and you'll have to throw it out and start over again (**Figure 10.6**).

5. Remove the gelatin from the microwave and you're now ready to proceed with your transfer process.

ADDITIVES—CAUTION!

Many of these processes involve adding additional materials to the gelatin mixture, including marble dust or graphite powder. These materials should be added only *after* heating the gelatin in the microwave. Many of these substances can cause severe reactions if heated in a microwave after mixing, and some can damage the microwave itself! Graphite conducts electricity when mixed in solution, and should *never* be placed in a microwave oven. If the mixture cools before you can use it, you can either carefully reheat it in a double boiler on an electric stove, in a slow cooker, or in an electric fondue pot (**Figure** 10.7). Or you can simply throw it out, clean the containers thoroughly, and start over. If you *do* reheat the mixture, make sure you have adequate ventilation, do not leave the mixture unattended, and be sure to keep it from boiling. Do not pour the mixture down the drain or you may clog up the plumbing. Scrape it onto newspaper and place it in the trash.

FIGURE 10.7 You can reheat gelatin safely using an electric fondue pot.

HINT: When mixing your gelatin, you should always use an adhesive in the mixture. Golden Polymer Medium, which you'll use in most of the processes in this book, acts as a binder or glue so that the mixture will adhere to the substrate. You can also use Talas Jade 403, a PVA white glue that will build a more solid surface than the plaster-like effect of the polymer medium. Changing the amount of marble powder you add will change the transparency. When mixing your gelatin for the specific processes in this section, as an alternative you can reduce the marble powder to just 1 tablespoon and replace the polymer medium with 2 tablespoons of Jade 403. The dried surface will look like ivory in both color and translucency. Afterwards, an ideal sealer for this variation is encaustic wax (see Chapter 22 on postcoats and Winter Aspen in the gallery of Chapter 16).

Pouring Gelatin onto a Surface

TOOLS NEEDED

⚠ Small plastic strainer

⚠ Rocket Blaster

There are a few tricks to pouring gelatin onto a surface or substrate that will help you minimize the bubbles and remove lumps. First and perhaps most obvious, be sure you're working on a level non-stick work surface. It's also important to pour the gelatin mixture when it's still about 100 degrees. If it's any cooler, it may not flow evenly across the panel; if it's any hotter, the adhesive on any tape you're using will release.

To pour the gelatin:

1. You'll use a small plastic strainer to guide the pour over the surface and to remove any bubbles or lumps during the pouring process. Place the strainer on the surface of your substrate, and slowly pour the gelatin mixture through it (**Figure 10.8**).

2. Move the strainer over the surface, guiding the pour, and using the bottom of the strainer itself to smooth the mixture out.

3. Guide the strainer out from the middle, towards the edges, but stay a bit away. After your substrate is mostly coated, guide the strainer right over the edge so that the gelatin flows cleanly off the surface (**Figure 10.9**).

4. Using your Rocket Blaster, gently pop any bubbles that have formed on the surface of your substrate (**Figure 10.10**).

HINT: As part of the processes, you'll need to test the gelatin mixtures to see if they've set up. To avoid damaging your image, you can pour a bit of the extra mixture onto the non-stick surface and test that instead of the substrate. You can also use your infrared thermometer on the surface, and do the transfer when it's about 65 degrees.

Salvaging a Substrate

Should you end up with a gelatin transfer that didn't turn out the way you expected, in many cases it's possible to salvage your substrate. This doesn't work for alcohol gel or SuperSauce—just the gelatin transfers. But you'll have to work fast. It's important to begin removing the gelatin before it dries and adheres to the surface.

Simply scrape off the gelatin using a plastic scraper or old credit card. Then mist the surface with water and use a paper towel to clean the surface of any remaining gelatin. Dispose of the ink-coated gelatin and allow the substrate to dry completely (at least a day) before reusing (**Figure 10.11**).

FIGURE 10.8 Pour the gelatin mixture onto the substrate using a small, plastic strainer.

FIGURE 10.9 Lifting the strainer off the surface of the substrate causes bubbles to form. To prevent bubbles, slide the strainer off the edge of the substrate.

FIGURE 10.10 Pop any bubbles using your Rocket Blaster (see Chapter 3 under "Other Tools").

FIGURE 10.11 Salvage a substrate by quickly scraping off the ink-coated gelatin before it has had time to dry.

Preparing a Panel

There are four types of panels that we'll use in the processes in this section: Baltic birch, Medex, plastic (polycarbonate or Plexiglas), and Econolite aluminum. Each of these different types of panels requires some basic preparation before you can use it for a transfer. See Chapter 2 for more information on these materials.

MATERIALS NEEDED	TOOLS NEEDED
⚠ Liquitex Gesso	⚠ 60-grit sandpaper
⚠ Golden Heavy Gel Medium	⚠ Tack cloth

HINT: If you'd like to include knotholes or surface defects as part of the character of your art, go right ahead! Just be aware that the gelatin may settle into the depression as it dries. Any defect in the wood will show on the surface after it dries.

To prepare a Baltic birch panel:

1. Cut your panel to size (12" squares for the examples in this book), making sure there are no knotholes or surface defects. Sand the edges to remove any burrs or splinters (**Figure 10.12**).

2. To ensure that your image is not distorted when you do the transfer, wet the panel thoroughly to raise the grain of the wood, and then set the panel aside and allow both sides to dry completely (**Figure 10.13**).

FIGURE 10.12 Sand the corners of your panel to make it smooth.

FIGURE 10.13 Raise the grain of the wood by wetting it thoroughly. This prevents image distortion during the transfer process.

3. Once the panel is dry, sand the edges and the front surface until the panel is smooth and clean, making sure that the edges and corners are slightly rounded (**Figure 10.14**).

4. After sanding, wipe the panel with a tack cloth to remove any sawdust. The panel must be completely clean and dry before proceeding or the mixture will not adhere properly (**Figure 10.15**).

To prepare a Medex panel:

1. Cut your panel to size (12" squares for the examples in this book), making sure there are no surface defects (again, unless you want them). Sand the edges to remove any burrs or splinters and route ¼" off the edges to provide a nice finish to the piece (**Figure 10.16**).

2. Sand the panel's front surface until it's smooth and clean, making sure that the edges and corners are slightly rounded (**Figure 10.17**).

FIGURE 10.14 Sand the panel and round the edges.

FIGURE 10.15 Clean the panel with a tack cloth.

FIGURE 10.16 This is a Medex panel with routed edges.

FIGURE 10.17 Sand the panel until it's clean.

FIGURE 10.18 Clean the panel well or your image won't stick.

FIGURE 10.19 Coat the back of the panel with gesso to keep it from warping.

3. After sanding, wipe the panel with a tack cloth to remove any sawdust. The panel must be completely clean and dry before proceeding or the mixture will not adhere properly (**Figure 10.18**).

4. Coat the back of the panel with undiluted white gesso to help prevent warping (**Figure 10.19**).

To prepare an Econolite aluminum panel:

1. Purchase a pre-sized Econolite panel or find a local sign shop to cut one to the correct size for you. As we learned in Chapter 2, it's difficult to cut metal yourself without creating burrs, nicks, or warps on the edges (**Figure 10.20**).

2. Sand the mill-finished surface with 60-grit sandpaper or scrub it with a wire brush to create a directional or random grain pattern (**Figure 10.21**).

FIGURE 10.20 An example of an Econolite panel.

FIGURE 10.21 Sand the panel using the correct tools.

3. Econolite panels have an oil coating on them from the factory, so wash your panel thoroughly with soapy water and then let it dry thoroughly (**Figure 10.22**).

4. As a final step, use your Heavy Gel Medium to seal the flutes (the openings between the corrugations) in the edges. Otherwise you may have gelatin flow inside and never dry out. This can cause dripping all over the gallery floor (as I found out the hard way) if the panel gets hot again. For some transfers I like to use wire cloth to score a pattern into the surface.

To prepare a plastic panel:

1. Remove the paper protective sheet from one side of the plastic panel.

2. Lightly sand the surface with the finest sandpaper you can find, or with 0000 steel wool. If you skip this step, the gelatin won't have anything to which to grip and will slide off the surface (**Figure 10.23**).

> HINT: The dust from the plastic may have a static cling, so it's a good idea to sand this in a different location from where you're going to be doing the transfer.

3. Use a tack cloth to remove all the dust from the panel, and proceed with your process (**Figure 10.24**).

FIGURE 10.22 Econolite with a scored pattern.

FIGURE 10.23 Sand the plastic panel in a different location from where you'll be doing the transfer.

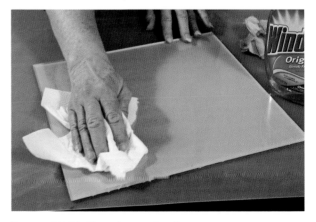

FIGURE 10.24 Clean the panel well.

11

WHITE MARBLE FRESCO TRANSFER

This project will create a digital fresco using the gelatin transfer process shown in the last chapter, and is a good first project to learn those techniques. The final image will have a wonderfully textured surface that looks like plaster.

After we complete the basic White Marble Fresco Transfer process, we'll tackle two variations: the Gelatin Glaze Layered Fresco and the White Fresco Distressed Print transfer processes. The first, more advanced process involves placing additional transparent or translucent layers onto the surface, so that parts of the underlying image show through.

The second variation creates an altered image by using handwork techniques with your own artistic tools. You'll learn how to manipulate and distress your printed image and even add additional pigment with watercolor paint to achieve a fine art finish.

Because many of these steps have to be done in advance, or when materials are at a critical temperature, make sure you read the entire process before beginning. As well, you should have read the introductory Chapter 10, along with Chapters 2 and 3.

About the White Marble Fresco Transfer Process

In the early 1990s, I began collaborating with two other artists, Dorothy Simpson Krause and Karin Schminke, with the goal of putting the artist's hand back into an inkjet print. Although our individual studios were located in Denver, Seattle, and Boston, we joined forces as Digital Atelier and worked together to develop this marble fresco transfer, which forms the basis for many of the transfer variations that I use today.

Over the course of our explorations, Dorothy, Karin, and I suffered through pots of rotting glue, failed experiments, and serendipitous accidents. Those experiments have led me to continue experimenting and inventing solutions to problems I often don't even know I have.

Here is the first of the marble fresco transfer processes. It should take you an hour to complete, not including image preparation time.

HINT: You can skip the marble powder if you'd like your image to be transparent, or use less to make a translucent, waxy appearing surface.

MATERIALS NEEDED

⚠ Digital image printed in reverse on DASS Transfer Film

⚠ One 12" x 12" x ½" Baltic birch wood panel

⚠ Prepared gelatin

⚠ ¼ to ½ cup white marble powder

⚠ 2 tablespoons Golden Polymer Medium (gloss)

TOOLS NEEDED

⚠ Safety equipment

⚠ Hard, smooth work surface

⚠ Fine-mesh strainer

⚠ Thermometer

⚠ Rocket Blaster

For a regularly updated product information list, check the book's website: www.digitalalchemybook.com.

To create a digital fresco using the white marble transfer process:

1. Prepare your digital image by printing it on transfer film. Make sure you leave enough trim to use the alignment board procedure described in Chapter 3.

2. Follow the instructions in Chapter 10 to prepare a Baltic birch panel. Make sure the panel is completely clean and dry.

3. Prepare the amount of gelatin that you'll use to complete the transfer according to the directions in Chapter 10.

4. After you've heated the gelatin in the microwave, remove it immediately and check its temperature. The mixture should be between 130 and 140 degrees.

5. To create the white fresco coating, add ¼ to ½ cup of white marble powder to the warm gelatin mixture and mix until the powder is completely absorbed. This powder is very fine, so take the precaution of wearing a filter mask (**Figure 11.1**).

   HINT: Stir slowly—never whisk—gelatin to avoid creating bubbles.

6. Add 2 tablespoons of polymer medium (gloss) and mix thoroughly (**Figure 11.2**).

7. Let the mixture cool at room temperature until it's about 100 degrees—do not put the mixture in a refrigerator (**Figure 11.3**).

FIGURE 11.1 Mix the marble powder into the warm gelatin.

FIGURE 11.2 Add the medium to your mixture.

FIGURE 11.3 Check the temperature of your mixture—you want it to be about 100 degrees.

FIGURE 11.4 Pour the mixture onto the panel through a strainer.

FIGURE 11.5 To fill gaps, lift the mixture onto the edges using an old credit card or spatula.

FIGURE 11.6 Check the panel's temperature to make sure it's cool enough to accept the image transfer.

8. Following the instructions in Chapter 10, apply the gelatin to your panel using a strainer to guide the pour (**Figure 11.4**).

> CAUTION: *Do not use tape to make a well for the gelatin mixture—you'll end up with a hard edge that ruins the fresco effect.*

9. Using an old credit card or spatula, pull some of the mixture onto the sides of the panel so that they're evenly coated. You can also lift some of the mixture back up to fill in any gaps on the panel, but you only have a few minutes to do this; once the mixture starts to set, any marks will show up in the final work (**Figure 11.5**).

Watch for a few minutes while it starts to set—as the mixture re-wets the panel, additional bubbles might form. Go ahead and pop them using your Rocket Blaster (if you skipped the wetting/drying/sanding steps when preparing the panel, you'll have a lot more bubbles to deal with since the grain of the wood will lift creating air pockets that will rise to the surface).

10. Gently touch some of the material that flowed onto your work surface, or carefully touch a corner of the panel (to avoid marring the surface). Once it's spongy and doesn't stick to your finger, it's ready to receive the image. At this point, it should be about 65 degrees or less. If you have a thermometer, you can use it to be sure it's ready. Then trim off the excess gelatin using an old credit card or spatula (**Figure 11.6**).

11. Following the instructions in Chapter 3, roll your print down onto the panel. Be careful not to let the last part flop down (**Figure 11.7**).

12. After three minutes, carefully peel the film off the panel as described in Chapter 3 (**Figure 11.8**).

13. Let the panel air dry at room temperature for a full day. If your room is warm or humid, you can use a fan to dry the panel faster, but make sure that the air blows up and across the print, not directly onto it (**Figure 11.9**).

14. As a final step, paint the edges of the panel or leave them white.

15. For display, insert four metal thumbtacks in the back of the panel and attach a wire so that the frame stands off the wall when hung. You can also use a floater canvas frame so that the natural fresco edge of the panel is exposed (**Figure 11.10**).

This work needs to be treated like an encaustic waxwork. Avoid exposing it to extreme high heat as the surface can soften. Under normal conditions you shouldn't have to worry about it.

FIGURE 11.7 Carefully roll the print onto the panel.

FIGURE 11.8 Remove the film from your panel.

FIGURE 11.9 You can speed the drying process using a fan if necessary.

FIGURE 11.10 Here I mounted the final print in a wooden frame.

FIGURE 11.11 This 12" x 12" white marble fresco transfer is titled *Anniversary*.

Gelatin Glaze Layered Fresco Transfer

This first variation is advanced because you'll place multiple layers onto your surface. The base layer is the white marble fresco, while each additional glaze layer is made from clear gelatin that allows the image underneath to show through. The result is a very hard, smooth surface. This process should take you about one hour for each layer plus one day of drying time between layers, not including image preparation time. We'll start this process assuming you've finished the white marble fresco transfer process (and you can choose to have it with or without an image at this point), and allowed the panel to dry completely.

MATERIALS NEEDED

- ▲ A completed white marble fresco
- ▲ Digital image(s) printed in reverse on DASS Transfer Film
- ▲ Prepared gelatin for each glaze layer
- ▲ 2 tablespoons Golden Self-Leveling Clear Gel for each glaze layer
- ▲ Instant coffee granules (optional)
- ▲ Dry pigments (optional)

TOOLS NEEDED

- ▲ Safety equipment
- ▲ Hard, smooth work surface
- ▲ Fine-mesh strainer
- ▲ Rocket Blaster

HINT: I use DASS Water Clear Pork Gelatin because it dries nearly crystal clear.

HINT: I use Golden Self-Leveling Clear Gel because it flows to a very flat, clear, and even surface that nearly looks like an epoxy resin.

To create a digital fresco using a gelatin glazed layer fresco transfer:

1. Using the white marble fresco process described earlier in this chapter, complete a white marble fresco panel with or without an image. Allow the fresco to dry completely before proceeding.

2. Prepare your digital image for each glaze layer that you wish to add by printing the image on transfer film. Make sure you leave enough trim to use the alignment board procedure described in Chapter 3.

3. Prepare the amount of gelatin that you'll use to complete the transfer according to the directions in Chapter 10, but only use 2 ½ teaspoons of gelatin per ½ cup of distilled water.

FIGURE 11.12 If you like, you can apply instant coffee granules to give your piece an interesting texture.

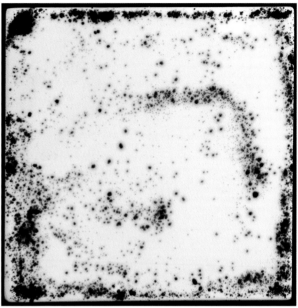

FIGURE 11.13 The panel stained with instant coffee granules.

4. After you've heated the gelatin in the microwave, remove it immediately and check its temperature. The mixture should be between 130 and 140 degrees.

5. Add 2 tablespoons of self-leveling gel and mix completely.

6. Let the mixture cool at room temperature until it's about 100 degrees—do not put the mixture in a refrigerator.

7. To create a more interesting surface, you can sprinkle instant coffee granules onto the surface (**Figure 11.12**). The instant coffee granules melt away, leaving random stains behind (**Figure 11.13**). But don't try this with regular coffee grounds—they won't dissolve.

8. Following the instructions in Chapter 10, apply the gelatin to your panel using a strainer to guide the pour (**Figure 11.14**).

9. Watch for a few minutes while the gelatin starts to set because bubbles might form. Go ahead and pop any bubbles using your Rocket Blaster.

FIGURE 11.14 Pour the gelatin glaze layer over the panel and coat it evenly.

FIGURE 11.15 Roll the print onto the panel.

FIGURE 11.16 Remove the film from the panel.

HINT: To create a colored base layer, you can mix powdered pigment into the fresco coating just as you would the instant coffee. Make sure you wear an adequate dust mask and eye protection when working with powdered pigments. You do this with either the white fresco or glaze layers.

10. Gently touch some of the material that flowed onto your work surface, or carefully touch a corner of the panel (to avoid marring the surface). Once it's spongy and doesn't stick to your finger, it's ready to receive the image. At this point, it should be about 65 degrees or less. If you have a thermometer, you can use it to be sure it's ready. Then trim off the excess gelatin using an old credit card or spatula.

11. Following the instructions in Chapter 3, roll your print down onto the panel. Be careful not to let the last part flop down (**Figure 11.15**).

12. After three minutes, carefully peel the film off the panel as described in Chapter 3 (**Figure 11.16**).

13. Let the panel air dry at room temperature for a full day. It's possible to have multiple layers with this technique. You can either transfer an image to the original opaque base layer or leave it blank. In either case, just continue to add additional layers of gelatin glaze, transfer the image, and let the panel dry completely between layers. You'll also need to use a high-quality water clear pork gelatin, and use as thin a layer as possible (which is why we use less gelatin) to keep the images crisp and avoid a yellow cast or blurring to the underlying layers.

14. As a final step, paint the edges of the panel or leave them white.

15. For display, insert four metal thumbtacks in the back of the panel and attach a wire so that the frame stands off the wall when hung. You can also use a floater canvas frame so that the natural fresco edge of the panel is exposed (**Figure 11.17**).

This work needs to be treated like an encaustic waxwork. Avoid exposing it to extreme high heat as the surface can soften. Under normal conditions you shouldn't have to worry about it.

FIGURE 11.17 This 12" x 12" gelatin glaze layered fresco on a Birch panel is titled *Cream Pitcher*.

VARIATION:
White Fresco Distressed Print Transfer

This final project is a fun one that allows you to express your own artistic voice. You'll manipulate the image printed on the transfer film to achieve a distressed appearance, and then follow the white marble fresco transfer instructions with your modified print. Be sure to allow extra time in this process for your image to dry after it has been altered. This basic process should take you about one hour to complete, not including image preparation time.

This process lets you use a variety of objects to create a pattern on the image's surface as you move the pigment around. This is where your artistic voice comes through—don't be afraid to experiment with different techniques to see what happens!

In addition to the tools and materials used in the basic fresco process above, you will need a few more tools.

To create a digital fresco using the white fresco distressed print transfer process:

1. Prepare your digital image by printing it in reverse on transfer film. Make sure you leave enough trim to use the alignment board procedure described in Chapter 3.

2. Using a spray bottle, lightly mist or sprinkle the inkside (the dull side) of the print with distilled water and allow it to sit for a moment to soften the emulsion (**Figure 11.18**).

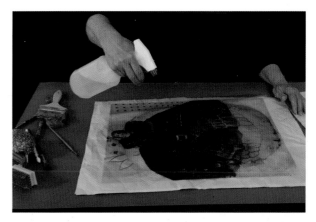

FIGURE 11.18 Spray the image lightly with a spray bottle and allow it to sit.

FIGURE 11.19 You can blot the image to remove some of the ink.

FIGURE 11.20 Brush and scrub the image with any tool you like. Now's your chance to get creative!

FIGURE 11.21 The final altered print after the distressing step.

3. To add an interesting effect, lay a piece of newsprint or other absorbent paper on top of the wet image and gently press it down. Pick up one corner and lift the paper off the image. You'll see that some of the ink has been removed (**Figure 11.19**).

    HINT: You can also use a sheet of unprinted cellophane for a slightly different look. Or you can try rice paper or other absorbent materials.

4. Using a wet brush, carefully work it across the image to move the pigment around. You can also use a dry brush to make coarse brush marks that bleed off the edge of the image, or draw on the image with watercolor crayons or Stibilo pencils. You can even use a wire brush, steel wool, or a razor and distress the image further. There's no right or wrong technique—follow your own spirit (**Figure 11.20**).

    HINT: Remember that the inks are process colors, so they do not mix the same as paint would—in other words, red and yellow do not make orange but rather some variation of gray.

5. Repeat these techniques until you've achieved your desired image, and then allow the altered image to dry (**Figure 11.21**).

6. At this point, the process is the same as the white marble fresco transfer process. Follow those steps to complete your image.

    These are two different final works, both made from the same digital image—the only difference is the distressing process used (**Figures 11.22** and **11.23**).

FIGURE 11.22 This 12" x 18" white fresco distressed print transfer is titled *Wash Dress I*.

FIGURE **11.23** This 12" x 18" white fresco distressed print transfer is titled *Wash Dress II*.

Conclusion

Keep in mind that no two transfers will be exactly alike, nor will the image be completely perfect; the cracks, distortions, and slight imperfections add value to the art and are part of the unique character of the work.

The classic fresco process formed the basis for my research and development of the digital fresco process. While some traditional artists might challenge the authenticity of this as a fresco, it really doesn't matter. The final work has the "fresco look," and both use pigment applied to a calcium carbonate (marble powder) surface. Just because an artist uses a digital brush doesn't mean the work is not every bit as artistic as works created using traditional techniques.

12

GELATIN ACRYLIC PAINT TRANSFER

Throughout my career, I've included the concept of layers in my artwork. This may have been multiple passes through an etching press or silkscreen, several layers of paint, or even a collage using cast paper. This concept exists in the digital world too—Photoshop includes layers as a core feature. I decided to try combining both kinds of layers to create a new and unique look to my work.

With this paint transfer process, it's your chance to get away from the computer and back into traditional media. You'll use your digital print as a guide and then create a unique *underpainting* on your substrate before transferring the image on top of it. Each work created this way will truly be one of a kind. No one can accuse you of just pushing the Print button to make the next copy. This process will take about an hour after you've created the painting.

Because many of these steps have to be done in advance—and others when materials are at a critical temperature in order to work properly—make sure you read the entire process before beginning. As well, you should have read the introductory Chapter 10, along with Chapters 2 and 3.

About the Gelatin Acrylic Paint Transfer Process

As we work through the steps and you get to the underpainting part of this tutorial, I encourage you to take as much time as you need with your traditional media—the painting you'll create is a substantial portion of the finished work.

So now let's get out your acrylic paints, brushes, and collage materials and get started. You'll rediscover how the accidents and experimentation that happen with real media change your perception of the computer. It's just another tool in your studio.

MATERIALS NEEDED

- Digital image printed in reverse on DASS Transfer Film
- 1 Medex panel with routed edge or ½" birch plywood panel sized for your image
- 2 tablespoons Golden Polymer Medium (gloss)
- Powdered pearlescent or mica material or paint with mica already included (assorted colors are available)
- Acrylic paint and brushes, collage materials (optional) to create your underpainting
- Isopropyl alcohol (optional)
- Prepared gelatin

TOOLS NEEDED

- Safety equipment
- Hard, smooth and level work surface
- Pencil
- Brushes for acrylic paint
- Blue painter's tape
- Thermometer
- Rocket Blaster

For a regularly updated product information list, check the book's website: www.digitalalchemybook.com.

To create an image using the gelatin acrylic paint transfer process:

1. Prepare your digital image by printing it on transfer film. Make sure you leave enough trim to use the alignment board procedure described in Chapter 3.

2. You can use either a Baltic birch or a Medex panel for this project. Instructions for preparing both types of panels can be found in Chapter 10. Since you'll put a thicker layer on the front surface though, you'll definitely need to paint the back side of either type of panel with undiluted acrylic paint to keep it from warping. Place your panel on your work surface (**Figure 12.1**).

3. Lay your image printed on the transfer film on top of the panel (you may want to tape it to the panel to hold it down). After looking at the image, determine where you'd like to have an underpainting, then reach underneath the film and trace those areas onto the panel in pencil. You can be as precise or spontaneous as necessary to suit your desired result. If you have multiple colors, you may want to pencil in a color code in that area—in other words, create your own paint by numbers! When you're done, remove the film from the panel (**Figure 12.2**).

4. After you decide where you'd like the first color, mix polymer medium (gloss) with the pearlescent powder (use appropriate safety precautions—this powder is very fine), or choose a premixed pearlescent paint or a straight acrylic paint, and then paint that area on the panel. In the example, I'm using an old brush to get very rough brush strokes (**Figure 12.3**).

FIGURE **12.1** Coat the back of the panel with acrylic paint to equalize the tension and keep it from warping.

FIGURE **12.2** Sketch the image on the panel.

FIGURE **12.3** Paint the first color on the panel.

FIGURE 12.4 Paint other colors on the panel.

FIGURE 12.5 Drip alcohol on wet paint to create patterns in the paint layer.

FIGURE 12.6 Form the well with blue painter's tape.

5. Continue to paint each area you've traced with the color that you would like to have in that location. You can add a bit of texture with the brush, which will show through in the final image. In **Figure 12.4**, I'm using white as my second color.

6. For an advanced look, you can drip isopropyl alcohol on the wet paint to create patterns in the wet paint layer, then either let it evaporate, wipe it off, or blot it dry with newsprint or an old towel. Each causes a different appearance in the dissolved paint (**Figure 12.5**).

7. Repeat these steps until you're satisfied with your panel, and then set it aside to dry completely.

8. Once the panel is dry, tape the edges of your panel with blue painter's tape. Make sure you press it firmly down to the edges—you want to form a well at least ½" deep. You can use duct tape on larger panels, as it sticks better and is less likely to leak (**Figure 12.6**).

> CAUTION: Mark the top of the panel and the top of your print after the panel is painted to make sure they align—once you pour the gelatin on top, you won't be able to see the paint until after it's dry. If you realize that you've rolled the print down wrong, before the gelatin dries completely, follow the instructions in Chapter 10 to salvage your substrate.

9. Prepare the amount of gelatin that you'll use to complete the transfer according to the directions in Chapter 10.

10. After you've heated the gelatin in the microwave, remove it immediately and check its temperature. The mixture should be between 130 and 140 degrees.

11. With your gelatin removed from the microwave, add 2 tablespoons of polymer medium (gloss) per batch and stir well. For the 24" x 24" panel in this example, I used six batches of gelatin (**Figure 12.7**).

12. Let the mixture cool at room temperature until it's about 100 degrees. Do not put the mixture in a refrigerator.

13. Following the instructions in Chapter 10, apply the gelatin to your panel using a strainer to guide the pour (**Figure 12.8**).

> *HINT: This is why it's so important to have a level work surface. You can add a wedge (or several) under the panel after the gelatin is poured if it didn't flow evenly, but you'll need to work quickly before the gelatin sets. If it doesn't work but is not yet dry, follow the instructions in Chapter 10 to salvage your substrate.*

14. Watch for a few minutes while the gelatin starts to set—as the mixture re-wets the panel, additional bubbles might form. Go ahead and pop them using your Rocket Blaster (if you're using a birch panel and skipped the wetting/drying/sanding steps when preparing the panel, you'll have a lot more bubbles to deal with since the grain of the wood will lift, creating air pockets that will rise to the surface).

FIGURE 12.7 Mix the polymer medium (gloss) into the warm gelatin.

FIGURE 12.8 Pour the gelatin mixture onto the panel.

FIGURE 12.9 Carefully roll the print onto the substrate.

15. Gently touch some of the material that flowed onto your work surface, or carefully touch a corner of the panel (to avoid marring the surface). Once it's spongy and doesn't stick to your finger, it's ready to receive the image. At this point, it should be about 65 degrees or less. If you have a thermometer, you can use it to be sure it's ready. You probably have plenty of time to let it cool—in the example shown, I waited two hours before transferring the image.

16. When it's cool, carefully remove the tape well—make sure you don't lift the gelatin away from the acrylic paint, or it won't adhere properly after the gelatin dries completely.

17. Make sure you align your print properly to the mark you made earlier—you probably can't see through the milky gelatin mix.

18. Following the instructions in Chapter 3, roll your print down onto the panel. Be careful not to let the last part flop down (**Figure 12.9**).

19. After three minutes, carefully peel the print off the panel as described in Chapter 3 (**Figure 12.10**).

20. Once it's fully removed, let the panel air dry at room temperature for up to two days. During the drying process, the gelatin will become clear and you'll be able to see your blended painted and digital image (**Figure 12.11**).

> *HINT: The underpainting can be made with any combination of collage materials, rice papers, and paint. Fully glue the materials to the surface with polymer medium and then let the surface dry completely before pouring on the gelatin layer. The liquid must fully cover the collage. After the gelatin dries, the image will fall into the texture of the collage materials.*

21. As a final step, you can paint the edges of your substrate the color of your choice, or if you're using a regular frame, simply frame the piece. I like to paint the routed edge with black so that my art floats in the frame.

22. For display of small panels, put in four metal thumbtacks in the back and attach a wire so it stands off the wall when hung.

This work needs to be treated like an encaustic waxwork. Avoid exposing it to extreme high heat as the surface can soften. Under normal conditions you shouldn't have to worry about it.

HINT: You can use this technique as a base layer under a gelatin glaze layer transfer (Chapter 11) in place of the white marble fresco layer. That's the cool part of these techniques—you can mix and match to reach your own creative objective!

FIGURE 12.10 Remove the film in the opposite direction you rolled it down.

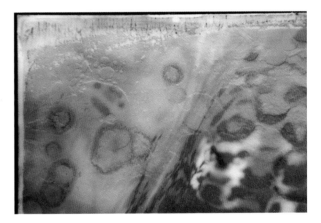

FIGURE 12.11 Detail of the upper left corner of the final image with clear, dry gelatin.

FIGURE 12.12 This 24" x 24" gelatin acrylic paint transfer is titled *Reflection Pool*.

Conclusion

The gelatin acrylic paint transfer process is a unique way of blending traditional art techniques and modern digital photography and imaging. Most of my own work is created using this type of hybrid method—bringing painting and printmaking into the 21st century.

I call myself an experimental artist—trying new things, and discovering what does and doesn't work is a lot of fun. Try experimenting by combining this technique with ones in the other chapters to create work that has layers, complexity, and depth. Create a painting, then find a photograph that fits, edit your images in Photoshop, and create a base layer painting from them—the sky's the limit!

13

TRAVERTINE TILE TRANSFER

Artists seem to enjoy merging high-tech with high-touch, and there's no better project for this than the travertine tile transfer. In this project, I will show you how to place your digital images directly onto natural rough tiles. Given the size of most tiles, this is an excellent project if you only have access to a desktop printer.

I like to select images that will complement the organic, earthy texture and color of the tiles. An old sepia photograph of a building or mountain would work well. Still life images can also be interesting, or even photographs of archeological sites or ancient ruins.

Because many of the steps in this project have to be done in advance—and others when materials are at a critical temperature in order to work properly—make sure you read the entire process before beginning. As well, you should have read the introductory Chapter 10, along with Chapters 2 and 3. This process should take you an hour to complete, not including image preparation time.

About the Travertine Tile Transfer Process

In this travertine tile transfer process, you'll apply the gelatin by dipping the tiles into the gelatin, rather than pouring the gelatin onto the tiles. You'll work with a few tiles in this procedure, but will still have enough gelatin to perform several transfers at once, so you may want to have extra images ready.

The tiles that you'll produce in this process are decorative, and should not be used for bathrooms, kitchens, floors or other places where food contact or physical wear is an issue. But don't let that stop you from building a room-side mural—once sealed, the tiles are plenty durable for people to look at and enjoy at any size!

HINT: Glazed tiles are slick and won't work. Highly polished stone, like granite, probably won't either—you need a natural rough finish. Tiles labeled "tumbled" have a rough surface and a nice natural edge.

HINT: If you prefer a glossy final look, use Golden Polymer Fluid Medium (gloss) instead of the fluid matte medium.

MATERIALS NEEDED

⚠ Digital images printed in reverse on DASS Transfer Film

⚠ Travertine, marble, or other porous stone tiles (I use 6" x 6" tiles in this example)

⚠ Enough gelatin to cover your tiles

⚠ Golden Polymer Medium (gloss)

⚠ Golden Fluid Matte Medium

⚠ Postcoat, such as Preserve Your Memories II

TOOLS NEEDED

⚠ Safety equipment

⚠ Hard, smooth work surface

⚠ Electric fondue pot

⚠ Heat protective gloves

⚠ Bristle brush

⚠ Metal scoop strainer or small spatula

⚠ Paper cup (or other stand to hold dripping tiles)

⚠ Rocket Blaster

HINT: Your fondue pot needs to be large enough to admit the flat side of the tiles you want to use, with room to safely dip the tiles (watch those sides— they're hot). For larger tiles, you can use a big double boiler turkey roaster. As always, make sure that either of these are used only for art. And make sure your appliance will maintain a temperature of 100 degrees.

To create an image using the travertine tile transfer process:

1. Prepare your digital image by printing it on transfer film. Make sure your image is large enough to extend over the edge of the tile.

2. The travertine tile is the surface onto which we'll be transferring the image. Most tiles can be used directly from the package, but if yours are dusty you can wipe them down with a damp cloth. If there are depressions with dust, a little canned air will blast them out. Make sure the tile is completely dry before proceeding (**Figure 13.1**).

3. Prepare one quart of gelatin (eight batches) in a single microwave-proof glass container as described in Chapter 10.

4. Heat the gelatin in the microwave, immediately remove it and carefully (it's hot!) pour the gelatin into the fondue pot. Set the pot to 100 degrees and wait for the temperature to stabilize (**Figure 13.2**).

5. To create the transfer layer, stir in 1 tablespoon of polymer medium (gloss) and 1 tablespoon of fluid matte medium per batch of gelatin.

6. Put on your heat protective gloves for the next steps.

7. Dip your bristle brush into the gelatin mixture and carefully scrub the surface of the tile with the brush. You want to work the mixture into all the cracks and holes in the tile to avoid air bubbles under the gelatin coating (**Figure 13.3**).

FIGURE 13.1 Travertine tiles come in many sizes and colors.

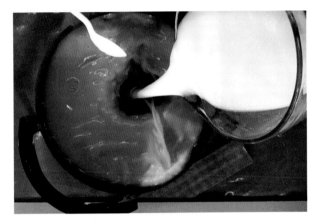

FIGURE 13.2 The fondue pot maintains the gelatin's temperature while you dip tiles.

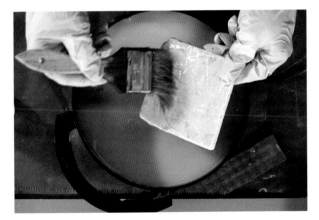

FIGURE 13.3 Brush the tile with warm gelatin to fill all the voids.

FIGURE 13.4 Carefully remove the tile from the pot.

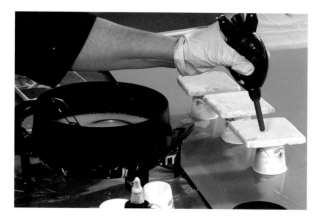

FIGURE 13.5 Let the tiles cool and drip on paper cups. Gently pop any bubbles.

FIGURE 13.6 Use both hands to roll the image down; don't let the film flop down.

8. Next, gently set the tile down into the fondue pot and leave it there for a few seconds, and then use your metal scoop strainer to lift the tile out. Be careful not to burn yourself on the edge of the pot (**Figure 13.4**)!

9. Without touching the top surface, set the tile onto a paper cup, and let it drip and cool. This will preserve the natural edge of the tile. If you see bubbles appear, gently pop them with your Rocket Blaster (**Figure 13.5**).

10. Once the gelatin has become firm to the touch, quickly repeat dipping all the tiles two more times to build a thicker smooth surface, while cooling them on the cup stands between each dip. Again, pop any bubbles that appear. Optionally, you can scoop out some warm gelatin and pour it over the tiles if you don't mind the mess of the run off.

11. Gently touch some of the material that dripped onto your work surface. Once it's spongy and doesn't stick to your finger, it's ready to receive the image. At this point, the surface should be cooled to about 65 degrees.

12. Following the instructions in Chapter 3, roll your print down onto the tile. Be careful not to let the last part flop down. Since you're not using an alignment board for these tiles, you will have to carefully line up the image to the edge of your tile as squarely as you can. If these are small tiles, start at one edge and use both hands to roll the film onto the gelatin (**Figure 13.6**).

13. After three minutes, carefully peel the film off the tile as described in Chapter 3 (**Figure 13.7**).

14. Once the film is fully removed, let the tiles air dry at room temperature for a full day. If you've used a high-quality gelatin, it will dry clear and the cracks and patterns in the tile will become integrated into the image (**Figure 13.8**).

15. These tiles really need a postcoat to protect them so that the ink won't run. Coat the tile lightly with a coating such as Preserve Your Memories II, which will make the tiles water resistant. Coat all six sides and edges if you plan to handle the tile a lot or if there's a risk that it will get wet (**Figure 13.9**).

16. Remember, this is artwork, and while you can install the tiles using traditional tiling techniques, they're not as durable as a fired glaze surface. Instead, I suggest using poster hangers (the kind with double-sided foam tape) to hang them directly on a wall without the need for a frame.

> *HINT:* If you want to use these as coasters, you can encase each tile in clear epoxy plastic resin (there are kits at your local hobby store). For decorative table art, apply cork pad to the back or display them on small easels.

FIGURE 13.7 Carefully remove the film from the tile.

FIGURE 13.8 The cracks in the surface are part of the image.

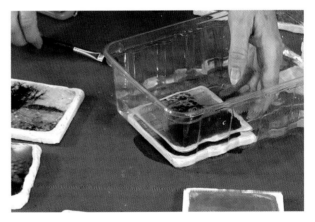

FIGURE 13.9 Without a postcoat, the ink would run when wet.

FIGURE 13.10 This is a selection of finished six-inch tiles with various titles.

Conclusion

The travertine tile transfer process is perfect for wedding photos (think of gifts for the wedding party), pictures of pets, cell phone snapshots, or vacation memories. I've found that everyone from fine artists to professional photographers, enthusiasts to crafters, really enjoy these tiles. Why put a snapshot in the same old frame again? Transfer it to a tile, display it on an easel, and create a conversation piece. Or, combine a collage of a dozen tiles into a mosaic as a centerpiece in you dining room. This is just a process. The image is your voice so speak softly or loudly with a massive installation.

14

GELATIN TRANSFER TO METAL

Have you ever walked along the ocean shore and noticed the effects of salt water on metal? Water, salt, and minerals all work in concert to create organic stains and patterns on the surface. Or have you ever seen an old barn's tin roof? Sun, rain, and snow also combine to give these objects a unique character—the signature of Mother Nature if you will. These surfaces inspired me to find a way to accelerate time and make my own antiquities for use in my artwork.

This process, like the others in this section, is a bit different—it's less about the transfer technique and more about creating a unique substrate, a substrate whose surface has been distressed as if Mother Nature was at work beside you. You can also use this process to transfer to clean metal, but I want to show how to create your own unique custom substrates that can enhance your image.

Because many of these steps have to be done in advance—and others when materials are at a critical temperature to work properly—make sure you read the entire process before beginning. As well, you should have read the introductory Chapter 10, along with Chapters 2 and 3.

About the Gelatin Transfer to Metal

In this project, I'll show you how to transfer an image to an Econolite metal panel. But first you'll change the character of the panel by distressing it. To accomplish this, you'll place scrap metal directly on the panel, and add salt and vinegar. Combined with the heat from the sun, the result will be patterns in your metal panel. The distressing process adds character to the final work, and gives you a chance to express your creativity. This is a messy process and it can generate some fumes, so I suggest doing the entire process outside. Not only is it well-ventilated outside, but you can hose down any runoff (pending your local regulations, of course).

Make sure you read and follow all safety labels on any products you use, and check for chemical reactions between any products you decide to try. If you're in doubt, don't do it. The products we'll use are generally safe, but you still need to follow good safety practices. I always wear eye protection, gloves, and a respirator when I'm doing this process. Once you've created your substrate, this process takes about an hour.

HINT: I prefer to use kosher cooking salt because I know it's free of any additives (road salt may have other chemicals in it).

MATERIALS NEEDED

⚠ An Econolite aluminum panel, cut to size

⚠ Plastic bag or drop cloth, large enough for your panel

⚠ Scrap copper, zinc, or other metal, clean and free of grease or contaminants

⚠ White vinegar (food grade)

⚠ Coarse salt

⚠ Enough gelatin to cover your panel

⚠ 2 tablespoons of Golden Polymer Medium (gloss) per batch of gelatin

⚠ Digital image printed in reverse on DASS Transfer Film

⚠ Masking tape

TOOLS NEEDED

⚠ Safety equipment

⚠ Random orbital sander

⚠ 60- to 300-grit sandpaper

⚠ Paint pad

⚠ Hard, smooth work surface

METAL SCRAPS

Different metals give different looks. Stainless steel is, well, stainless and may not do much at all! Metal recycle centers have an abundance of industry leftovers, as do scrap or junkyards. You're looking for pieces that will make interesting patterns on the Econolite panel as the metal reacts. Just be careful that there isn't any oil, grease, or other residue on the metal scraps, and that they are pure metal (no vinyl, rubber, fabric, etc.). We're going to be using vinegar and salt on them and you want to avoid any reactions. If you're not sure, it's better to look for something else and be safe. After making several trips out to my local metal recycler's salvage yard, he now knows me and calls when he gets the "good stuff."

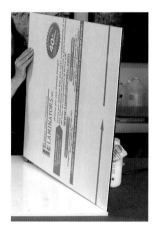

FIGURE 14.1 Your panel as it's ready to prepare.

To create a transfer to distressed metal:

1. Follow the instructions in Chapter 10 to prepare an Econolite panel. Sand the entire surface with a random orbital sander. This opens up the surface of the metal so that it will be easier to chemically age. If you skip this step, you will not get much patina. The coarser the sand paper, the more aging you will get (**Figures 14.1** and **14.2**).

   > HINT: If you sand the panel by hand, you'll likely end up with a noticeable pattern. If that's your artistic goal, that's fine, but just make sure you've evenly abraded the surface for the next steps.

2. Place a large clear plastic sheet or plastic bag on a table that can handle any runoff from the distressing process. You can also do this outdoors (I used my driveway the first time). Place the Econolite panel in the center of the sheet.

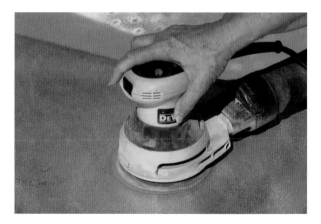

FIGURE 14.2 Sand your panel to get a better patina.

FIGURE 14.3 Place metal scraps to create an artistic appearance and then add salt and vinegar.

FIGURE 14.4 Wrap your panel and let it age in the sun.

FIGURE 14.5 Carefully unwrap your panel.

3. Now place your scrap metals on the panel's surface; the end result is that stains and pitting will appear on your panel. Arrange the scraps to create interesting patterns and shapes (though you won't know exactly how it turns out until it's done). Copper scraps make dark stains, and other metals create other colors. The longer the metals are in contact with your panel, the more pitting occurs. Sprinkle coarse salt over the surface, and then pour enough vinegar on the surface to dampen the salt and the panel (**Figure 14.3**).

> *CAUTION:* Don't use a spray bottle to apply the vinegar—it's nasty if you breathe it in. I recommend doing this outside to avoid any fumes in your studio as the panel bakes.

4. Without moving the scraps, wrap up the panel and scraps in the plastic sheet, or close the plastic bag loosely (don't seal it—you want it to dry out), and let it cook in the sun for several days. The longer it bakes, the deeper the pits will be. From now on, wear gloves to handle the panel to avoid fingerprints on your image later on (**Figure 14.4**).

5. After the metal panel and scraps are completely dry, unwrap the package and carefully lift off the scrap metal. If the panel has not aged enough, sprinkle on more vinegar and rewrap the scraps for another day (the salt won't have evaporated, so you don't need any more). Once you like the effect, it's time to clean the panel (**Figure 14.5**).

FIGURE 14.6 Careful with the runoff when you wash your panel.

FIGURE 14.7 You'll use a photograph of the panel to help visualize your final work as you create your digital image.

6. Use hot soapy water to wash off the residue, and then rinse the panel with clear water and allow it to dry. Be careful with the residue—it's not good for shrubs, trees, pets, children, your lungs, or your lunch (**Figure 14.6**).

    > *HINT:* Subject to local regulations, a drive-way is a great place for this step.

7. Take a digital photograph of the panel; you'll need it to help visualize the final work as you create the digital file that will be transferred (**Figure 14.7**). *This is very important to do before you move on to the next step!*

8. Now you need to coat the panel with an adhesion layer. Spread a thin coating of undiluted polymer medium (gloss) across the surface using the paint pad (**Figure 14.8**). Make sure you move in both directions and rub it lightly into the surface. This also will seal the metal so no further oxidation will occur. Let the panel dry completely (over-night is a good idea).

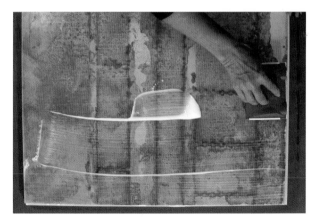

FIGURE 14.8 Make sure the coating of polymer medium (gloss) is thin and even.

FIGURE 14.9 This is the digital file, without the photograph of the substrate. The image is flipped so that it later transfers properly.

FIGURE 14.10 Paint areas of the panel to achieve your vision.

9. This process requires that you create your substrate before you complete your final digital image. This is the fun part. I try to tip the scale to the natural surface. Try to use the least amount of photographic image to add to what nature has created. Make the viewer guess what is real and what is nature made. Follow the procedures in Chapter 3 under "Computers and Software" to combine your image with a photograph of your substrate so that you can visualize your final work while you create your digital image. Remember, you're only printing your new image, and not the layer with the photograph of the substrate (**Figure 14.9**).

10. Prepare your digital image by printing it on transfer film. Make sure you leave enough trim to use the alignment board procedure in Chapter 3.

11. Place the print on the panel, check to make sure that the image registers properly, and then set it aside. The metal has just a medium gray value so to increase the contrast in an area that might be the center of interest, you can add white acrylic paint to it. Paint any areas on the panel that you might want to be a brighter color (**Figure 14.10**). If you'd like to hide the brush strokes, you can mist the paint slightly with water. Let it dry, then place the print back over the panel and repeat until all the underpainting is completed.

> *HINT: You can use the techniques in Chapter 12 to trace areas to paint, and even use pearlescent paints or pigments mixed with gesso on these panels. If you mix white paint with your medium, the medium will become translucent and let some of the substrate show through. Let your creative voice speak!*

12. Using your masking tape, tape the edges of the panel to form a well at least ½" deep. For larger panels, use duct tape or multiple layers of wide masking tape. Press the edges firmly down to prevent leaks. At least ½" of the tape should wrap under the back side (**Figure 14.11**).

13. Prepare the gelatin that you'll use to complete the transfer as described in Chapter 10. Make enough to cover the entire panel. For the 24" x 24" panel (four square feet) in the illustrations, I used six batches of gelatin.

14. After you've heated the gelatin in the microwave, remove it immediately and check its temperature. The mixture should be between 130 and 140 degrees.

15. To create the transfer layer, stir in 2 tablespoons of polymer medium (gloss) per batch of gelatin, and allow it to cool to 100 degrees (**Figure 14.12**).

16. Mark the top of the panel so that you know how to align the print for the transfer. Following the instructions in Chapter 3, prepare your film and alignment board.

17. Following the instructions in Chapter 10, apply the gelatin to your panel using a strainer to guide the pour (**Figure 14.13**).

> *HINT: In my own work, this distressing process has lead to a series called* Illusion *and you can find an example of this work titled* Organic Replication *in the gallery in Chapter 24 (or see www.lhotka.com for other images in that series).* Organic Replication *was created using the distressed to metal process as its base. I used stretched woven copper cloth as my substrate. It looks fragile, as if it could dry up and fall apart at any moment. When I exhibited this piece, viewers were drawn closer to the surface, trying to identify the image against the substrate. The longer someone is captured by my work, the better I've done my job.*

FIGURE 14.11 Make sure you have a tight seal when creating your tape well.

FIGURE 14.12 To avoid bubbles, always stir, never whisk when you add a substance to gelatin.

FIGURE 14.13 Be careful not to move the tape when pouring the gelatin.

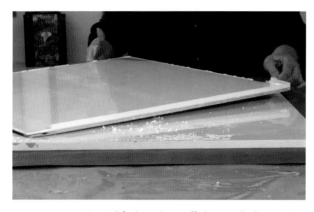

FIGURE 14.14 Don't lift the gelatin off the panel when removing the tape.

FIGURE 14.15 Make sure you have the panel aligned, and then roll down your print.

FIGURE 14.16 Remove the film from your panel.

18. If you see bubbles appear, gently pop them with your Rocket Blaster. Allow the gelatin to cool to 65 degrees. Once cool, carefully remove the tape by pulling it outward and down. Don't let the gelatin layer lift up from the surface, or you won't get good adhesion for the final print (**Figure 14.14**). If you turn the panel, make sure you keep track of the top, since the gelatin will look white and will cover up the image on the panel.

19. Following the instructions in Chapter 3, slowly roll your print down onto the panel. Be careful not to let the last part flop down (**Figure 14.15**).

20. After three minutes, carefully peel the film off the panel as described in Chapter 3 (**Figure 14.16**).

21. Once the film is fully removed, let the panel air dry at room temperature for a full day. If your room is warm or humid, you can use a fan to dry the panel faster, but make sure that the air blows up and across the print, not directly onto it. As the gelatin dries, your image will "develop" and the gelatin will become transparent. The first time I created a blended photo this way, I stayed around all day watching the gelatin clarify (with my fingers crossed!).

22. Wait a full two weeks so that the gelatin coating dries completely and you don't seal in moisture before mounting or finishing.

23. The panel can easily be framed with any standard molding. I create much of my current work on metal panels, since I've found that current collectors prefer art and photographs that can be displayed without glass.

24. This work needs to be treated like an encaustic waxwork. Avoid exposing it to extreme high heat as the surface can soften. Under normal conditions you shouldn't have to worry about it.

Conclusion

One of the criticisms of digital art is that there isn't a uniqueness to it because each image can be printed over and over. This project is a direct challenge to that assumption. The creation of your own custom substrate, and its integration with your digital file, all bring your own hand to the high-tech world.

FIGURE 14.17 The title of this 24" x 24" gelatin transfer to metal is *Ivy*.

15

CLEAR GELATIN TRANSFER TO PLASTIC SHEET

n this project, you'll create a translucent panel by transferring a digital image to a thick sheet of clear acrylic, polycarbonate, or Plexiglas. I use this process to create images with both a virtual and physical sense of depth. I'll create my image in Photoshop, using many different layers. Then I'll print the composite image and do a single transfer to a sheet of plastic. Or, I might split the image and print part of it on regular inkjet paper to place behind the plastic sheet. For an added twist, I sometimes use translucent plastic and then backlight the image, simulating how it actually looks on a computer screen. This clear gelatin transfer to a plastic sheet results in a cracked surface that looks like old leather, and adds an interesting texture that highlights these different layering techniques.

Because many of these steps have to be done in advance or when materials are at a critical temperature, be sure to read the entire process before beginning. As well, you should have read the introductory Chapter 10, along with Chapters 2 and 3. This process should take you two to four hours to complete, not including image preparation time.

About the Gelatin Transfer to a Plastic Sheet

Presentation, though a key part of creating a work of art, is often overlooked. Sometimes you want a classic appearance so you use a wood frame, while other times you might use a black metal frame for a clean, elegant appearance. On the occasion where you want a more contemporary presentation, you can mount your image using edge grip standoffs, fasteners that let the work float unframed on the wall. The problem, however, is if you were to mount the work under glass it would be too heavy. But as you'll see in this process, by placing the image directly on a sheet of plastic we can have the best of both worlds: a durable presentation that doesn't weigh too much when mounted.

The resulting work has a sense of substance and allows the viewer to approach the art on a personal level. Simply printing on paper doesn't create the same experience. Plastic sheets like this can also be backlit, creating a whole new dimension of possibilities.

In this process, you'll first add different dilutions of polymer medium to your plastic panel to create an uneven surface, later followed by a coating of gelatin on to which you'll apply your digital image.

HINT: *The plastic sheet needs to be at least ¼" thick.*

MATERIALS NEEDED

- ⚠ Digital image printed in reverse on DASS Transfer Film
- ⚠ A sheet of clear plastic, acrylic, or Plexiglas
- ⚠ Golden Polymer Medium (gloss)
- ⚠ Paste wax postcoat

TOOLS NEEDED

- ⚠ Safety equipment
- ⚠ 60-grit sandpaper
- ⚠ Hard, smooth work surface
- ⚠ Sponge roller
- ⚠ Fan
- ⚠ Brush
- ⚠ Blue painter's tape or duct tape

For a regularly updated product information list, check the book's website: www.digitalalchemybook.com.

To create a transfer using the clear gelatin to plastic process:

1. Prepare your digital image by printing it on transfer film. Make sure you leave enough trim to use the alignment board procedure described in Chapter 3.

2. Follow the instructions in Chapter 10 to prepare a plastic panel. You'll also need to sand the edges and corners because the piece will be hung frameless on the wall. Make sure the panel is completely clean and dry before proceeding (**Figures 15.1** and **15.2**).

3. After sanding and cleaning the panel, pour some of your polymer medium (gloss) into a separate container and dilute it with water at a ratio of one part water to three parts medium. Your goal is to end up with an uneven coating of medium on the panel, so pour both the diluted and undiluted medium onto different portions of the panel and push it around with a brush (**Figure 15.3**).

FIGURE 15.1 Sand the corners since you won't use a frame.

FIGURE 15.2 Rinse and dry the panel completely.

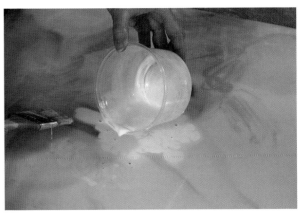

FIGURE 15.3 Create an unusual and uneven coating of polymer medium (gloss) on your panel.

FIGURE 15.4 Cracks will begin to form after about two hours of drying.

4. Point a fan directly at the wet surface and let the panel dry overnight. After a few hours, you'll see the medium dry up and form a cracked surface. When it's dry, you should have a beautiful patterned substrate (**Figures 15.4** and **15.5**).

5. Create a tape well on the panel using blue painter's tape or duct tape (**Figure 15.6**). Since plastic can be hard to stick to, you may need multiple layers of painter's tape. Or you can use duct tape which is plenty sticky in just one layer (after all, it's like The Force: it binds the universe together).

6. Prepare the amount of gelatin that you'll use to complete the transfer according to the directions in Chapter 10. For the 24" x 24" sheet in this example, I used six batches of gelatin.

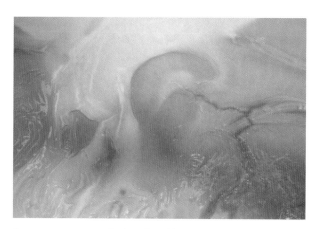

FIGURE 15.5 A cracked surface like this adds texture to the art.

FIGURE 15.6 Make sure the tape sticks nice and tight to the plastic.

7. After you've heated the gelatin in the microwave, remove it immediately and check its temperature. The mixture should be between 130 and 140 degrees.

8. Add two tablespoons of polymer medium (gloss) per batch of gelatin, and mix completely (**Figure 15.7**).

9. Let the mixture cool at room temperature until it's about 100 degrees. Do not put the mixture in a refrigerator.

10. Following the instructions in Chapter 10, apply the gelatin to your panel (**Figure 15.8**).

11. Because of the uneven surface, you may need to help the gelatin cover the high points. Use a stiff brush to scrub the warm gelatin into the cracks of the acrylic medium (**Figure 15.9**).

FIGURE 15.7 To avoid bubbles, stir, don't blend, the mixture.

FIGURE 15.8 Be careful not to break the tape well when you pour the mixture.

FIGURE 15.9 Scrub the gelatin into the surface with a brush.

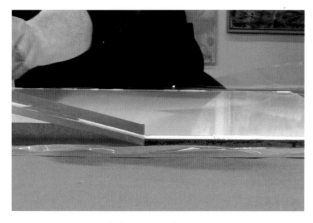

FIGURE 15.10 Carefully remove the tape.

12. Allow the gelatin to cool to 65 degrees. When cool, carefully remove the tape by pulling it outward and down. Don't let the gelatin layer lift up from the surface or you won't get good adhesion for the final print. If you turn the panel, make sure you keep track of the top, since the gelatin will look white and cover up the image on the panel (**Figure 15.10**).

13. Following the instructions in Chapter 3, roll your print down onto the panel. Be careful not to let the last part flop down (**Figure 15.11**).

14. After three minutes, carefully peel the print off the panel as described in Chapter 3 (**Figure 15.12**).

15. Once it's fully removed, let the panel air dry at room temperature for two weeks—it takes that long for the acrylic medium to dry completely.

FIGURE 15.11 Make sure you have the panel aligned, then roll down your print.

FIGURE 15.12 Remove the film from your panel.

16. If you'd like, you can use very fine finishing sandpaper and, either by hand or with an electric sander, selectively sand away parts of the image (**Figure 15.13**).

> *HINT:* A random orbital sander will give you an even appearance, while hand sanding with a rotary or band sander will create swirls or grain in the work. Make sure you take appropriate safety precautions when sanding the panel.

17. Since it takes acrylic polymer medium so long to fully dry, I recommend waiting a few weeks before sealing the surface. I like to use a paste wax to finish these works (**Figure 15.14**).

18. Once it's dry, place a sheet of white paper or a mirror behind the image if you prefer a traditional frame. This will help highlight the image and provide a deep, rich look. Or, if you're going to hang it with edge grip mounts, you can paint the back (I use black, silver, or white, but you can use any color).

FIGURE 15.13 Sand the image to achieve your creative vision.

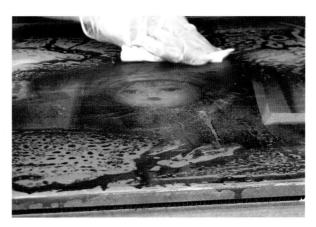

FIGURE 15.14 After the surface is completely dry, gently apply the wax.

FIGURE 15.15 The title of this 24" x 24" clear transfer to plastic is *Red Window*.

Conclusion

Keep in mind that no two transfers will be exactly alike, nor will the image be completely perfect; the cracks, distortions, and slight imperfections add value to the art, and are part of the unique character of the work.

Transferring an image to a thick, plastic sheet is a modern approach to presenting a traditional photographic image. It is suitable for mixed media, digital collage, or fine photography. As you move up to larger sizes, it can be a bit of a challenge to handle the panel, and you may need an assistant to help pour the gelatin and roll down the print. In the summer, it's hard to get the gelatin to set, while in the winter, it may set before it flows across a large panel! I actually plan what work I'm going to do during the year based on the weather. Eventually, I may add a candy-making table that can be both heated and chilled, but that's a luxury that will have to wait for the future!

16

GALLERY OF WORK: GELATIN TRANSFERS

Amber

32" x 32". White Marble Fresco Transfer. For this image, the leaf was placed in water, frozen, and then photographed. I used less marble powder in this fresco so it would have a more translucent look like quartz. To enhance that stone-like effect, I added quartz crystals to the gelatin coating. After the piece was dry, I sealed and polished it with paste wax.

Land Quilt

40" x 64". Gelatin Glaze Layered Fresco Transfer to Baltic Birch Tiles. I made plaster molds to mimic the patterns of aerial photographs, and then photographed the molds and applied color in Photoshop. I used a laser to cut the birch into 8" x 8" squares, which gives a clean cut but with a wonderful, burned edge. I painted both sides of the tiles with black gesso, avoiding the burned edge, and then dipped the tiles in the white fresco mixture so that both sides were coated. The burned wood stained the fresco mix as it dried to create random patterns. Once dry, the tiles were photographed and combined into a single image in Photoshop. I masked or erased parts of the image in Photoshop so that the final tiles would have areas with either no image, or only a faint image. This is a good example of how to make large art from a desktop printer by stitching together smaller transfers.

Land Road

14" x 20". Gelatin Glaze Layered Transfer Process to Baltic Birch Box. I photographed the surface of the patterns formed on a black box that had been dipped in the white marble fresco mixture, and then combined that photograph with a landscape photograph in Photoshop to distort and add texture to the image.

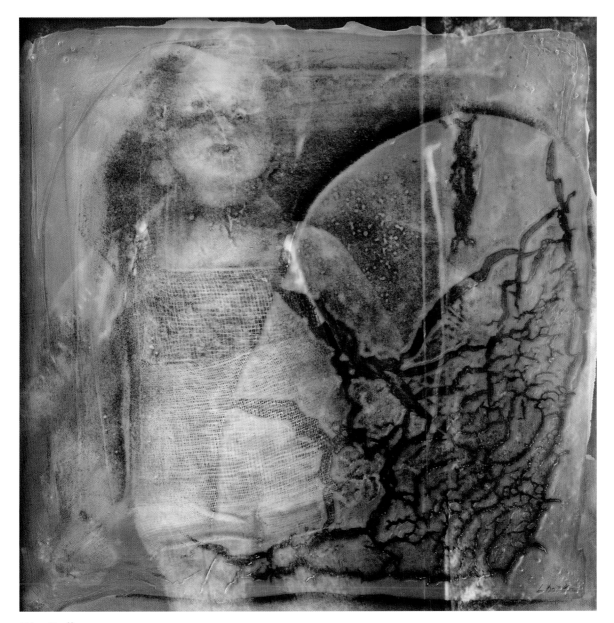

Dirt Doll

24" x 24". Clear Gelatin Transfer to Plastic Sheet (Polycarbonate). I sanded and washed the polycarbonate, and then poured polymer medium (gloss) onto its surface. I intentionally dried the surface quickly with a fan causing the medium to shrink and crack before pouring clear gelatin onto the surface and completing the transfer. After allowing the work to dry for two weeks, I sanded the surface to remove portions of the image. I printed a second image of the same file on white paper and placed it behind the polycarbonate sheet that shows through the sanded area giving depth to the image. I sealed the piece with paste wax.

Winter Aspen

24" x 30". White Marble Fresco Transfer to a Baltic Birch Box. Instead of using polymer medium (gloss) in the fresco recipe, I substituted double the amount of white glue, and used only half the amount of marble powder. After applying the transfer, the image dried to a very hard translucent surface. I then painted the surface with hot encaustic wax, and placed the box in the hot sun to liquefy the entire surface. When there was a nice even puddle of wax I carried it inside to cool, and the next day, buffed the surface to a glass-like surface.

Underground

6" x 6". Travertine Marble Tile Transfer. In Photoshop, I combined a landscape photograph with a scan of the bottom of a rusty tin can. Then, using a desktop inkjet printer, I printed the image and transferred it to a tile dipped in the gelatin mixture, allowed it to dry, and sealed it with a postcoat. I wanted to display it on a table, so I used self-adhesive cork disks on the back.

Fruit Basket

12" x 12". White Marble Fresco Transfer to Medex Panel. On a recent visit to my local woodworker, I snagged a large bag of hardwood sawdust that looks similar in consistency to the marble powder frescos. Because it was wood dust, I used rabbit skin glue instead of gelatin. This made the mixture too thick to use with a strainer, so I just poured it onto the panel. The end result is an image that looks like it was printed on milk chocolate with a suede-like finish.

Poppy Field

24" x 24". White Marble Fresco Transfer to Econolite Panel. I sanded the mill-finished side of the panel with very coarse sand paper to create a surface to which the gelatin mixture could bond. I used just 2 tablespoons of marble powder for each batch of gelatin mixture so the gelatin layer would be translucent and allow a bit of the metal to show through. I also added quartz crystals to the gelatin mixture to enhance the stone-like effect.

Potted Plant

24" x 30". White Marble Fresco Transfer to Baltic Birch. After I printed several images to film, I cut them up and then placed the film pieces on the gelatin mixture. When you use several photographs, this is a more spontaneous approach to composing an image collage.

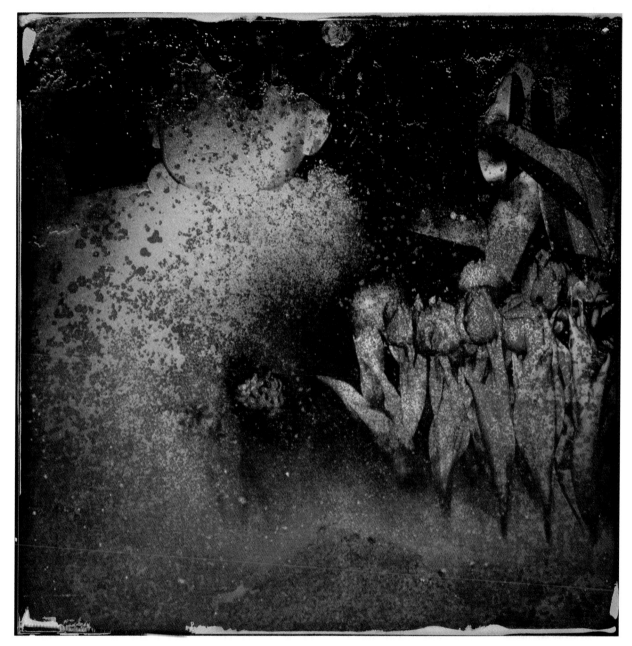

Pyrite

32" x 32". Clear Gelatin Transfer to Glass. I am currently developing this process to transfer an image to glass. After the transfer, I coated the back with 24K gold leaf. I used a chemical to eat part of it away and then I back painted the piece with red acrylic paint. The red shows through when viewed from the smooth glass side.

DIRECT PRINTING

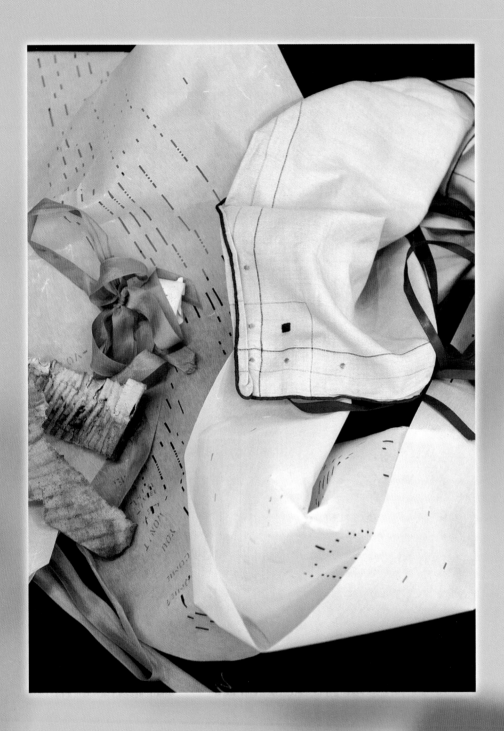

17

INTRODUCTION TO DIRECT PRINTING

To this point in the book, I've talked all about the transfer process. With *direct printing*, you create a unique substrate and print onto it directly—no transfer involved. It's just like printing a letter or document, but you're printing onto a different surface, your customized substrate.

Direct printing onto a custom substrate brings together your skills as a photographer, a collage artist, and a painter. Creating your custom substrate can involve building a collage, a procedure that can be as elaborate as you choose to make it. Or if this sounds too daunting, it can be as modest as taking silk or tissue paper and a few paints, and creating a work of art to use as a base image. Alternatively, and for the simplest of paths, you can direct print to metal with a desktop printer and just skip the collage steps altogether.

The important question becomes, How thick a substrate can you safely put through your printer? There are some desktop and wide-format models that can print to interesting surfaces, but there are also a number that can't, so it's very important that you read your printer's manual to make sure you can do these processes on your printer.

For a regularly updated product information list, check the book's website: www.digitalalchemybook.com.

Special Tools

Printer manufacturers never envisioned their customers using custom substrates, so there are some special tools you need to do so safely. When you apply a precoat to any of the wide variety of substrates, you'll choose from several styles of coating tools for the job. Some of these tools you can make yourself, and I'll show you how to make one of them, a coating rod. After you've created your substrate, you can test that it fits through your printer with an inexpensive tool you'll make called a slot ruler. This is something I use every time I run a custom substrate through one of my printers—it's cheap insurance to make sure the substrate will fit properly.

Coating Tools

When you direct print onto any substrate (even if it's just a bare sheet of metal), you apply an inkjet precoat to the surface so the ink does not soak into or run off the surface (see Chapter 2). You add the precoats with a coating rod, bar, or sponge brush. For smooth surfaces like sheets of metal, I use a coating rod that gives me perfectly even coverage of the precoat. For surfaces with texture, I use a coating bar with a soft nap pad that fills in the small imperfections and spreads quickly and evenly before it starts to dry. I save the sponge brushes for very small works; these brushes don't coat as evenly and too much of the precoat soaks into the brush.

If you're working on a small smooth surface, the first set of procedures outlined in this chapter shows you how to make a simple and inexpensive coating rod. In the second set of procedures, you'll apply a test precoat to see how well your new coating rod works.

If you want a longer rod, I recommend buying a Mayer rod rather than trying to make your own. In any case, the rod that you use should be one to two inches wider than the substrate you're coating. See Chapter 3 for more detail on coating rods, including the Mayer rod.

> **MATERIALS NEEDED**
>
> ⚠ One 7/16"- 14 solid steel all-thread-plated 12-inch rod
>
> ⚠ 16-gauge solid copper wire
>
> ⚠ Double-sided tape
>
> ⚠ Precoat

HINT: Many rods are not plated, meaning they will rust, and some have a rough edge on the threads that prevents the precoat from releasing properly. This is why I wrap the threads with smooth copper wire. Make sure you get a rod that is zinc-plated (or galvanized), and has even threads running from end to end. Stainless steel or brass rods are more expensive but work very well. You can use a different diameter as long as the threads are listed as 14.

To make your own coating rod:

1. You'll need to use a rod that is as straight as possible, and has threads that are at an even depth. Usually, one side of a rod is more even than the other. Place the rod on a flat table, and look at the gap between the table and the rod. Roll the rod back and forth until you find the position that has the most threads touching the table. Then mark the rod at each end so that you know that's the part you will place on the substrate as you're using it (**Figure 17.1**).

2. Wrap the copper wire around one end of the rod, and tightly roll the rod as you push the copper wire into the thread. The wire is stiff, so make sure you keep it tight to the rod as you wrap it—the good news is that once it's on, it'll just stay in place by itself. The ends of the wire need to be on the top of the rod (the side that doesn't touch the substrate). This will also help you to see which side of the rod you should keep down on the substrate (**Figure 17.2**).

The next set of procedures show you how to apply a precoat to a substrate. Follow these steps to test how evenly the precoat applies as you use your new coating rod. If the rod doesn't coat evenly, your wire is not tight enough in the threads.

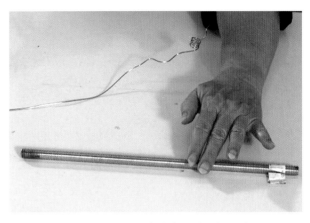

FIGURE 17.1 Test the rod to find the side where the most threads touch the table.

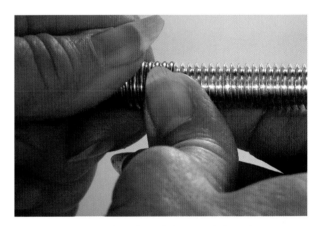

FIGURE 17.2 Wrap the wire tightly around the rod, pressing it into the threads.

To apply a precoat to a substrate:

1. Attach a few strips of double-sided tape to the back side of your substrate, and then press the substrate to your work surface.

2. If you're using a coating rod, apply a thick line of the precoat to your work surface *above* the top of your substrate. Place your coating rod above that line and draw the rod across your substrate in one smooth motion. Make sure you hold the rod still without twisting—draw it, don't roll it (**Figure 17.3**).

3. If you're using a coating bar, apply a thick line of precoat *directly to* your substrate, and then lightly spread it across the entire substrate with the coating bar. Make sure that your last run across the substrate is in one direction only so that you remove any excess precoat and leave an even, smooth layer.

Slot Ruler

To make sure your substrate is not too thick to pass through your printer, I invented a tool called a *slot ruler*. It consists of two tubes with a space between them that matches your printer's platen gap. When you slide your substrate between the tubes, you verify that your substrate is not too thick for your printer. I can't use my caliper for this test because it can't reach into the center of a large substrate; I use my caliper instead to check the thickness of the base material before I start adding to the substrate (**Figure 17.4**).

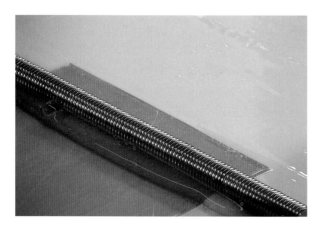

FIGURE 17.3 Draw the coating rod across your substrate.

FIGURE 17.4 To avoid head strikes, use your slot ruler to test your substrates before printing on them.

CAUTION: Head strikes are bad—they damage print heads and budgets. To reduce the risk of having a head strike, you should always pass your custom substrates through a slot ruler before printing on the surface. Since we'll build a slot ruler that is no thicker than your platen gap, you should have a margin of safety. Refer to Chapter 3 for information on printer platen gaps and media tolerance for various printers.

CAUTION: Check that the tubes you use for your slot ruler are straight and even, since you'll rely on them to test substrates. Place them on a flat table and check all four sides. If you can see light between the tube and the table, they're bent.

MATERIALS NEEDED

▲ Two 1" x 1" square, aluminum tubes

▲ Double-sided tape

▲ New U.S. coins

▲ Masking tape

TOOLS NEEDED

▲ Caliper

To make your own slot ruler:

1. Cut your tubes to be two inches wider than your printer's width. If your printer is wider than 24", use tubing with a larger cross-sectional area to ensure that the tubes are rigid.

2. You need to insert a spacer between the tubes that is no thicker than your platen gap. You can use either coins (see the "English and Metric Units" sidebar in Chapter 2) or washers to do this. In either case, check the thickness of your spacer with your caliper.

3. Use very thin double-sided tape to tape the spacers between the two tubes (**Figure 17.5**).

4. Apply masking tape around the tubes and spacers to keep the stack together. This tape is just used to keep it from shifting—the double-sided tape holds the spacers in place.

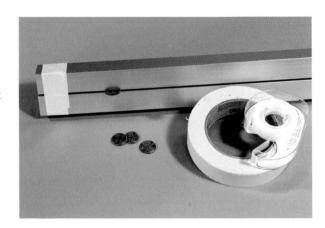

FIGURE 17.5 Some of the materials for making a slot ruler.

FIGURE 17.6 A substrate is smashed as it goes through a laminator.

FIGURE 17.7 A brute force tool to smash substrates.

Smashing Collaged Substrates

So what do you do if your collaged substrate is a bit too thick? You smash it! You can use a hand-operated laminator to press the substrate evenly flat. I have one from Pacific Mount that is 26 inches wide, so it's perfect for a 24-inch wide carrier sheet. Since it's hand operated, it's fairly inexpensive—if you're doing a lot of mixed media digital work, it's well worth the investment. Of course, if your base panel (the panel you started with) is too thick, you're out of luck (**Figure 17.6**).

Another alternative is to use a steel brayer. I had a local tool shop make mine for me—it weighs 50 pounds and is 10 inches wide and 6 inches in diameter. This works best if your substrate collage is still damp—once it's dry, it's harder to smash. Place the substrate on a hard smooth surface (the floor works just fine), cover it with plastic, and roll the brayer over the surface. If it's still too thick, well, I've been known to use a hammer on stubborn spots until it fits safely through my slot ruler (**Figure 17.7**)!

Collage Materials and Substrates

I prefer to make my custom substrates first, and then seek out an image that matches, but you certainly can do the reverse. So how do you go about creating a custom substrate? To start, you can collect all sorts of old books, fabrics, bits, and pieces of interesting material, scraps, and ephemera. I like to run as green an operation as I can, so this is a good use of torn up old paintings or prints that didn't quite work out as I'd hoped (**Figure 17.8**).

If your collage is strong and flat enough, you can print directly onto it. Otherwise, you can use a carrier sheet (see Chapters 2 and 20) as a base to build your collage, apply an inkjet precoat (see Chapter 2), print onto it, and then remove it from the carrier sheet.

FIGURE 17.8 Collect collage materials from anywhere you find them.

In other processes in this section, the sheet that you're using to carry the collage remains part of the final artwork. You'll use a sheet of metal, plastic, paper, or other synthetic material as a base and then add paint and material to that surface before direct printing onto it. If you choose clear plastic, you can have a transparent base that you can backlight, or place an assemblage or second collage behind it.

Because most printers need to see white to load materials (gray or other colors won't work), you can use a spunbonded polyester felt-like fabric in white to support substrates as they print. Pellon interfacing from a fabric store is also white and will work well. It's sold in some art supply stores as a pastel cloth. Another option is to use gray landscape fabric to which you apply a light coat of white paint.

Of course, you can do all of the processes in this section without the collage steps; then it's just a simple direct printing procedure. Just follow the instructions for each substrate and omit the collage steps. One of the easiest is to select a ridged sheet of metal or plastic that is thin enough to feed through your printer, prepare it, and then print directly onto the surface. These processes let you get the look of an expensive print shop print on your home equipment.

HINT: For desktop printers you should have three inches of white material at the beginning of a substrate in order to load the material properly. You should also use a one-inch white margin on each edge for these printers. Wide format printers need that same three inches of white material on the leading edge, and also need three inches of white material on each side of the substrate to load properly.

HINT: I always do a nozzle check or test pattern (see your printer's manual for instructions) before printing on a custom substrate to make sure I don't have a clogged print head. The extra step is well worth it—re-creating a substrate takes time!

SPECIAL CAUTION: PRECOATS AND YOUR SUBSTRATE

If you apply any precoat to an unsanded, shiny, or smooth metal surface, you run the risk of the precoat coming off the substrate and damaging your printer as you print. With some products, this can happen even on a sanded surface, so be very careful when choosing a precoat.

Let the substrate dry for several days; some precoats detach very easily or even lift off on their own when completely dry. Then test them on a small project and on an inexpensive printer before trying a large print on your precious wide format machine.

I specifically developed the DASS Universal Precoat to reduce the risk of the substrate detaching, and it's what I use for all the processes in this book and on the enclosed DVD. I highly recommend that you take special care with these processes regardless of what precoat you use, and even additional care if you use a different precoat than those I cover in this book. I've tested many of them, and haven't found another that is as 'universal' as the one I developed.

Printing using a Template

There are two challenges when direct printing onto a substrate. The first, as I've pointed out, is that most printers need a white surface to begin feeding a substrate. The second is that they cannot properly print full bleed directly onto custom substrates. To address both issues, you'll create a template to use around your panels. This procedure should take you no more than about 15 minutes, and what's more, you'll be able to reuse this template for many prints so long as it's in good condition.

For this example, I'm using an Epson 3880 printer and want a full-bleed print. You'll need to create a template out of mat board, but first you need to do a test run of the image placement. Your dialog box settings may be slightly different than those for my Epson and my Mac.

To create a template for panels:

1. Cut a sheet of white mat board (2-ply for desktop printers, 4-ply for wide format printers) to be at least two inches wider than your metal panel, and several inches longer (I use 17" x 30" for my 13" x 19" panel).

2. Look at the back of your printer to see how high the feed slot is. Create a platform (either temporary or permanent) that's the same height as the bottom of the slot, and then slowly slide your mat board in. If you get a paper error, try again. Once it's in, put a piece of blue painter's tape as a marker on the back of the printer at each edge of the mat board to ensure that you feed the final print in the exact same place. Congratulations, you've just created a home-made flatbed printer.

3. In Photoshop's Print Settings dialog box, click Print Setup, and then under Print Settings, select Paper Size/Manage Custom Size and create a custom paper size that's the same size as your mat board, with margins of zero (**Figure 17.9**).

4. From the Page Setup pull-down menu, select Manual-Rear as your feed. From the Media Type pull-down menu, select Watercolor Paper Radiant White or another watercolor paper. Set your Color Mode to Off, and your Output Resolution to SuperPhoto 1440 dpi or the highest resolution for your printer.

5. Either in the print dialog box or on the printer itself (like the Epson 3880), set the platen gap to its widest setting.

> CAUTION: *Some print drivers reset the platen gap after every print, and there's no way to stop it. So make sure you check that setting every time before you print. You may damage your printer if you forget to do this! Make sure you read your printer manual and follow all instructions included.*

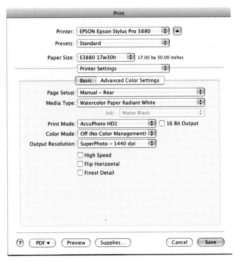

FIGURE 17.9 The Print dialog box settings for my Epson 3880.

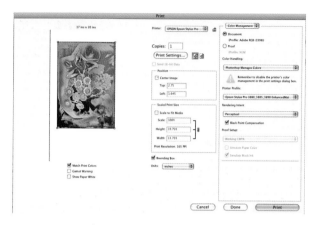

FIGURE 17.10 The Print settings in Photoshop CS4.

FIGURE 17.11 Partially print the mat board.

FIGURE 17.12 Draw around your panel on the mat board.

6. In Photoshop's Print dialog box, center the image on the page, but uncheck the Center Image option. Change the Position Top to be 2.75" (most printers require a margin like this when feeding flat media), and set the color options as you usually do for your system (**Figure 17.10**).

7. In the Print dialog box under Color Management, select your document profile, and under Printer Profile, select a matte printer profile (I used the Epson Stylus Pro 3880_3885_3890 Enhanced-MattePaper in this example). Under Rendering Intent, I selected Perceptual and checked Black Point Compensation.

   As I mentioned earlier in the book, color management is a complex topic, so your settings may vary slightly from mine. A major reason to choose a thick paper is so that the platen gap is set wide.

8. Print the image, and allow it to run until you can see where the image is printing. Once you see both edges and a couple of inches of print, you can cancel the print to save ink. Eject the mat board and allow it to dry (**Figure 17.11**).

9. Place the metal panel on the mat board so that it's just above the edge of the start of the print and centered between the two edges. Make sure it's centered on your mat board, and then draw a line around the panel with your pencil (**Figure 17.12**).

   HINT: *The 4-ply mat board is too thick for the printer shown here. Both the mat board and your metal panel have to safely fit through your printer.*

10. Take the metal off of the board and set it aside. Watch your fingers when working with the panel— no fingerprints! Use a ruler and single-edge razor or mat knife to cut out the center of the board. I like to cut it slightly large so that the metal will drop in easily (**Figure 17.13**).

11. Place the metal panel face down in the mat board, and then tape around the edges to hold it in place. Tape a second layer to give added support. Turn the board over and brush off any lint or dust with a soft brush—remember, don't use your hand or you'll make fingerprints (**Figure 17.14**).

12. Use your canned air to do one last dusting on the surface, and then feed the combined metal and template into the back of your printer. Make sure you slide it between the two pieces of blue tape that you'd earlier placed on the back of the printer (**Figure 17.15**).

13. Print your image the same as you did for the earlier test in Step 8. When it's out, set it aside to dry for a bit. You can see that the image bleeds off the metal and onto the template (**Figure 17.16**).

FIGURE **17.13** Remove the center of the mat board.

FIGURE **17.14** Tape the panel into the mat board template.

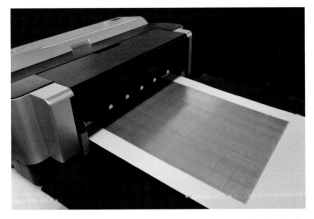

FIGURE **17.15** Load the metal and template into the back of your printer. Remember to set the platen gap on the printer!

FIGURE **17.16** A fresh print, bleeding off the edge of the metal.

WIDE FORMAT PRINTER TIPS FOR EPSON PRINTERS

If you're printing on a wide format printer, there are some additional steps you should follow.

If your machine will handle it, use a 4-ply mat board instead of the 2-ply to help hold the larger panels.

Place a sheet of foam core behind the printer to help provide support for the panel and template (**Figure** 17.17).

Make sure that you have sufficient clearance on the bottom side of these printers for your image and the template to come out without hitting the floor (**Figure** 17.18).

You can also move the printer against a wall so that the wall supports the template.

FIGURE 17.17 Support larger panels as they feed into and out of the printer.

FIGURE 17.18 Think about supporting your image on both ends of the print.

Conclusion

As I write this book (September 2010), I'm actively working on extending these processes, and am finding new techniques every week. Some of the pictures you'll see in the gallery are the products of those experiments (things that aren't ready to publish yet), and you'll even see a few tips in this section that are recent discoveries. They are so cool I've included them here as things for you to experiment with. You can always check the book's website, www.digitalalchemybook.com, for the latest errata and updates.

18

DIRECT PRINTING ONTO METAL

A rtists seek to express primal energies in their work, much like ancient alchemists exploring the fundamental building blocks of nature. Metal has a warmth and glow that makes it an ideal medium for artistic expression, yet the same properties that make it attractive also make it difficult to use—especially when leveraging modern digital printing techniques. With a few simple steps however, you can prepare the surface to receive images far more complex and artistically interesting than traditional techniques allow.

Although the techniques in this direct print onto metal process can be used on a variety of types of sheet metal, you'll work with simple mill-finished aluminum, found at any hardware store or home center. Please note that it is important to use metal that is 0.03 inch thick or less.

With this project, you'll work with both wide format and desktop printers. Since direct imaging onto these types of substrates can damage your printers if not done properly, read Chapters 2, 3, and 17 before proceeding. Follow the information regarding platen gaps, testing, and squashing substrates, and understand your printer's limitations and capabilities. If in doubt, don't risk your hardware.

Please read through all of the instructions before beginning the procedures below so that you have the items you need already prepared.

About Direct Printing onto Metal

Printing on metal is something that many digital artists want to do, but it's a tricky business. I have periods of time where I'm able to direct print many projects onto metal at once without any problems, and other times where nothing seems to work right. That's why it's so expensive at the service outlets—there can be a lot of waste if you're not careful. Take this slowly, and make sure you understand the limitations of what can be achieved. In some cases, you may need to embrace some imperfections as artistic variation, and shift the goal line. This has led me to accept accidents and do more experimenting, which is how I developed this process; in the end, the problems become artistic challenges.

HINT: Read the "Special Caution" sidebar in Chapter 17 before you use a different precoat.

CAUTION! Before you begin, make sure your printer will take material this thick—read your manual, measure the materials, and check everything twice. Head strikes are bad! When in doubt, don't print.

MATERIALS NEEDED

⚠ Metal sheet no thicker than 0.03 inches (the example in this process is 13" x 19" sheet)

⚠ Inkjet precoat (I use DASS Universal Precoat in this example)

⚠ 2-ply white mat board for most desktop printers or 4-ply for most wide format printers

TOOLS NEEDED

⚠ Safety equipment

⚠ Hard, smooth work surface

⚠ Protective gloves

⚠ 220-grit sandpaper

⚠ Random orbital sander (optional)

⚠ Long metal ruler

⚠ Drywall sanding screen

⚠ 1" x 2" board as long as your substrate

⚠ Mat knife or single-edged razor

⚠ Masking tape

⚠ Rocket Blaster or canned air

To direct print onto metal:

1. Prepare your digital image by setting it to be ½" to 1" larger than your metal panel.

2. For this example, I'm using a 13" x 19" 0.025" thick sheet of mill-finished aluminum. This comes with a protective plastic sheet on one side that must be removed. Make sure that once it's off, you never touch the metal with your bare hands—the fingerprints will show in the final image even if you try to sand them off. I wear nitrile or nyplex gloves when I handle these (**Figure 18.1**).

3. Wrap a piece of 220-grit sandpaper around a piece of wood, foam board, or sanding pad, and lightly sand the surface of the metal using a circular motion. This gives the coating something to bind to (**Figure 18.2**).

4. I like to have a grain in my metal panels (and so have chosen an image that will work with that surface). Take a piece of drywall sanding screen and wrap it around a block of wood (**Figure 18.3**). Then place a 1" x 2" board parallel to one edge and draw the sanding screen back and forth several times to create a grain (**Figure 18.4**).

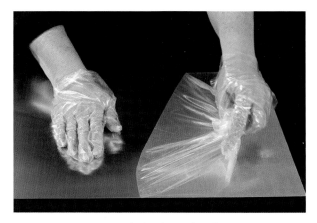

FIGURE 18.1 Don't touch the sheet after the protective plastic is removed.

FIGURE 18.2 Carefully sand your panel.

FIGURE 18.3 Wrap drywall sanding screen around a block of wood.

FIGURE 18.4 Draw the screen across the panel to create a grain.

5. Keep moving the board across the surface, and repeat the sanding process. You can rotate the panel 90 degrees and continue if you'd like a hatched surface rather than a linear grain (**Figure 18.5**).

6. Wash the metal to remove all of the metal dust, dry it completely, and then place it on pieces of foam, wood, or other wedges to keep it slightly off your non-stick work surface.

    HINT: You can use a random orbital sander for Step 3 and then skip Steps 4 and 5, which will give you a sparkly finish rather than a grain-like one.

7. Using one of the coating applicators from Chapter 3, thoroughly apply a coating of your precoat to the entire surface of the metal. If you discover you missed some of the surface after it's dry, you can apply a second coat, but since it will partially dissolve the first, you may not get as good a result. Make sure you draw the coating across the surface in a single direction, and that it's evenly coated with no ridges or globs. The precoat adheres to the sanded surface and creates a satin-like surface. Make sure the coating dries completely before printing on it (**Figure 18.6**).

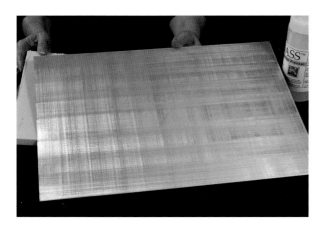

FIGURE 18.5 Create a cross-grained panel if you like that effect.

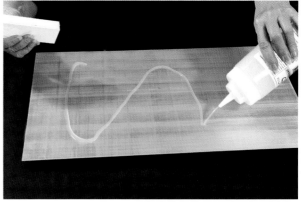

FIGURE 18.6 Apply your precoat to your substrate.

8. Follow the steps in Chapter 17 for printing with a template to print your image onto your substrate. Make sure you set your platen gap (**Figure 18.7**)!

9. Carefully lift out your print. You can reuse the template for other prints, but just make sure it's dry and that the edges of the cutout haven't swelled with too much ink (**Figure 18.8**).

10. Depending on which precoat you used, the ink may be tacky for several days. I like the Universal precoat because the ink dries to a light touch in a few minutes. Rabbit skin glue takes longer to dry. In any case, no matter how dry it feels, allow the panel to sit for three to seven days before applying a postcoat and before framing it. Pigment inks have a solvent that needs to gas out before you seal the surface.

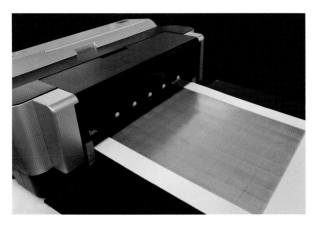

FIGURE 18.7 Load the metal and template into the back of your printer. Remember to set the platen gap on the printer!

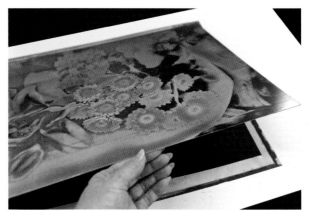

FIGURE 18.8 You still cannot touch the metal surface with your fingers.

EXPERIMENTAL TECHNIQUE

As I write this book, I'm experimenting with a new technique, and it's so cool that I had to share it even at this stage. I've found a way to print directly onto a very slick, shiny, smooth surface, which allows me to reuse the metal if the print is not right!

First, clean your metal with a lint-free cloth and isopropyl alcohol (no need to sand it first). Let it dry completely (in a well-ventilated area), and then coat the surface with Old World Art Gold Leaf Adhesive using a sponge brush or coating bar. This primer coat (applied before a precoat) sticks to the metal to allow your precoat to bind to it, and remains water clear when dry. Once it's dry, it will be tacky, but clear. Apply your inkjet coating, and if you use a paint pad or spreading bar to apply it, you can get good coverage with just a single layer. The dry precoat will not delaminate! And it dries crystal clear (**Figure 18.9**).

FIGURE 18.9 Old World Art Gold Leaf Adhesive works as a clear primer.

Let the inkjet coating dry completely, and then print as you would with the direct print to metal process. It appears (at this early stage of my testing this process) that if your print fails, you can wash off the ink and precoat under cool running water, leaving the adhesive behind. Once your metal and adhesive are dry, the surface will be tacky and clear again, so you can just apply the precoat, and print again. If this continues to work as it appears, this would really reduce the cost of lost prints! It also should work on other non-porous surfaces, so it's an area I'm continuing to experiment with.

Since this is an experimental technique, take any and all precautions when trying it out. You can also check the book's website, www.digitalalchemybook. com, for any updates.

FIGURE 18.10 The title of this 13" x 19" direct print onto metal is *Basket Weave*.

Conclusion

This kind of metal preparation makes the image appear to be printed on a woven satin metal cloth, with a semi-gloss sheen. If you've hand-sanded it, any dust specks or irregular areas will look like they are an intentional part of the work.

When an image is printed on metal, it glows and just shimmers. That look is why so many people are attracted to it, but the techniques haven't been available for most artists and photographers. Now everyone with access to an inkjet printer that has an appropriate platen gap can try it out. Professional photographers and artists—myself included—are just beginning to discover how printing on metal can bring a whole new dimension to their work.

19

DIRECT PRINTING ONTO METAL LEAF

One of my favorite metals to work with is copper. I find that it glows with warmth and has a rich luster that adds an almost elemental quality to my work. I became hooked on it, and developed the SuperSauce transfer process (see Chapter 6) so that I could use real copper clad sheets I found in a salvage yard.

I wanted to try direct printing, but unfortunately most copper is either too heavy or too soft to properly feed through a printer—even if you mount it or smash it flat. I know from experience, and I regret my attempts! After searching for another option, I finally set out to replicate my own copper substrate by making an imitation copper clad sheet, and that's what I'll teach you to do in this process, along with a variation for those who want to do more (**Figure 19.1**).

Please read through all of the instructions before beginning the procedures in this chapter so that the items you need are already prepared.

FIGURE 19.1 Not exactly something you want to feed into your printer.

About Direct Printing onto Metal Leaf

Pre-made copper clad substrates are created from fiberglass laminates, epoxy resin, and woven glass cloth that are then coated with copper. Unfortunately, these commercial substrates are too thick to use, so I've created this method to make my own.

We'll start with raw fiberglass laminate (also known as circuit board material), which is usually labeled G10 or F4, and available from most plastic supply stores (**Figure 19.2**). Some of the material is so thin you can see through it, almost like a light fog, and the colors range from off white and amber to pale green. I find this to be a wonderful base for experimental inkjet printing because it's stiff and it's thin, available in 0.01" thickness. Because it stays flat, it will feed through desktop printers with a back feed slot like the Epson 3880. In this process, you'll use the Chapter 17 technique for printing using a template so that the printer recognizes and loads your substrate.

FIGURE **19.2** G10 fiberglass laminate is translucent.

CAUTION: Take all appropriate precautions when cutting these materials. I prefer to have mine cut at the store where I buy it. Likewise, take appropriate safety precautions when working with any fiberglass.

MATERIALS NEEDED

- G10 or F4 fiberglass resin circuit board material
- Cleaning supplies (laundry detergent, Windex, trisodium phosphate, or soap and water)
- Old World Art Gold Leaf Adhesive
- Genuine Copper Leaf
- Inkjet precoat

TOOLS NEEDED

- Safety equipment
- Hard, smooth work surface
- Paint pad or spreading bar
- Cotton balls
- Double-sided tape

For a regularly updated product information list, check the book's website: www.digitalalchemybook.com.

To create a direct print onto metal leaf:

1. Prepare your digital image by setting it to be ½" to 1" larger than your metal panel.

2. The edges of your material may be sharp, so I always wear protective gloves. Clean your circuit board material using your chosen supplies. Make sure that the oil is completely removed; otherwise the coatings won't stick to the surface. Do not sand the surface as that will create fiberglass dust.

3. Use a paint pad or spreading bar to apply an even coat of your Old World Art Gold Leaf Adhesive to your panel. Clean the tools immediately with soap and water (**Figure 19.3**).

   HINT: This is really sticky stuff, so I recommend using a disposable paint pad since you may not be able to get it completely clean.

4. Wait until the surface is dry and tacky (about 30 minutes). Tear off a sheet of Genuine Copper Leaf, keeping the tissue on top, and then float the leaf down. After the leaf touches the adhesive, take off the tissue (**Figure 19.4**).

   HINT: You can also use other metal leaf, including aluminum and gold, or even a mixture of several metals.

FIGURE 19.3 Spread an even coat of adhesive on your panel.

FIGURE 19.4 Cover your panel in copper leaf.

FIGURE 19.5 Polish the leaf with cotton balls—sweep up the scraps and dispose of them properly!

FIGURE 19.6 Load the metal and template into the back of your printer. Remember to set the platen gap on the printer!

5. After you apply all of the leaf, buff it down with cotton balls. Keep going until you remove all of the excess leaf and the remaining surface is smooth and polished. Collect the scraps and dispose of them properly. You can print on either side of this surface (since the leaf is visible through the fiberglass), but for this example we'll print directly onto the metal leaf (**Figure 19.5**).

6. Using one of the coating applicators from Chapter 3, thoroughly apply a coating of your precoat to the metal. If necessary, you can apply a second coating, but because it will partially dissolve the first, you may not get as good a result. Make sure you draw the coating across the surface in a single direction, and that it's evenly coated with no ridges or globs. Let each coating dry completely before adding another layer or printing on it.

7. Follow the steps in Chapter 17 for printing with a template to print your image on your substrate. Make sure you set your platen gap (**Figure 19.6**)!

8. Carefully lift out your print. You can reuse the template for other prints, but just make sure it's dry and that the edges of the cutout haven't swelled with too much ink.

9. Depending on which precoat you used, the ink may be tacky for several days. No matter how dry it feels, allow the panel to sit for three to seven days before applying a postcoat and before framing it. Pigment inks have a solvent that needs to gas out before you seal the surface.

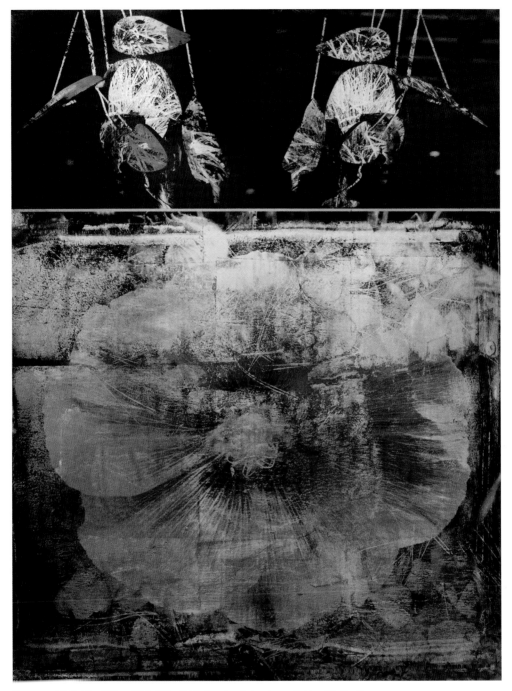

FIGURE 19.7 The title of this 18" x 24" direct print onto metal leaf is *Brothers*.

Variation:
Direct Printing onto Aluminum Foil

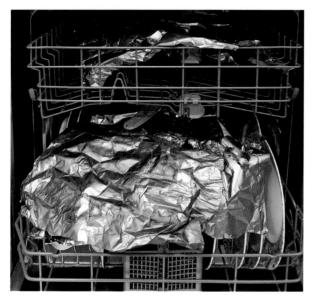

FIGURE 19.8 Use a dishwasher to prepare clean, new foil.

Now I'll show you a more advanced variation. As I mentioned before, I grew up in the Midwest, and have a miser streak that I inherited from my mom. She used to wash disposable pie tins and reuse them. One day I got a crazy idea to wash aluminum foil in the same way. Well, it didn't turn out to be reusable for food, but after I was done picking the pieces out from among the dishes, I decided to try using it in my art, and loaded up my dishwasher with another batch (**Figure 19.8**)!

As you might guess, this foil is very fragile, so you'll use a different kind of substrate, YUPO synthetic paper made from polypropylene pellets to lay the aluminum on. Yupo paper is recyclable, waterproof, and tree-free. Most art supply stores and some paper stores sell it. I like to use the Legion paper versions in opaque and translucent white. Use the heaviest paper you can find (as long as it still fits through your slot ruler).

HINT: Only Rhoplex N580 acrylic emulsion works for this process. This product is a stronger pressure sensitive adhesive than Old World Art Gold Leaf Adhesive. It holds down the heavier foil and is also a strong enough adhesive if you wish to add additional rice paper collage to parts of the substrate.

MATERIALS NEEDED

- YUPO white synthetic paper
- Rhoplex N580 acrylic emulsion
- Washed regular weight aluminum foil (use the dry cycle, and a good detergent)
- Inkjet precoat (this example uses DASS Universal Precoat)
- Pellon or spunbonded polyester fabric

TOOLS NEEDED

- Safety equipment
- Hard, smooth work surface
- Foam brush
- Brayer
- Foam insulation
- Plastic bag
- Double-sided tape

Since the printer isn't able to recognize and load a collage substrate with the dark aluminum foil, we'll use a spunbonded polyester or Pellon fabric as a carrier sheet three inches wider on each side and with a three inch leader for the printer to recognize and load.

> HINT: The Epson wide format printers have a vacuum platen that holds the media flat. This feature eliminates the need for the pizza wheels found on smaller printers. Pellon fabric works well with this system because the air passes through the open-weave fabric allowing the vacuum platen to pull the custom media flat.

FIGURE 19.9 Paint two coats of acrylic emulsion onto your synthetic paper surface.

To create a direct print on aluminum foil:

1. Prepare your digital image by setting it to be ½" to 1" larger than your paper.

2. Place your synthetic paper on your work surface, and use a foam brush to apply a smooth, even coating of the acrylic emulsion. Let it dry and then apply a second coating in the opposite direction. Since the synthetic paper doesn't absorb moisture, it will stay flat in the printer (**Figure 19.9**).

3. The acrylic emulsion remains tacky when it's dry (after about 30 to 60 minutes) forming a pressure sensitive adhesive. Once it's in this state, you can start laying the washed foil on the surface. In **Figure 19.10**, I'm only covering part of the surface, but you can cover it all if you'd like.

FIGURE 19.10 Apply foil in interesting patterns to your coated YUPO surface.

> HINT: Rhoplex N580 is similar to the adhesive we used in the metal leaf process, but is stronger and becomes a clear, pressure-sensitive adhesive. It's very important that you cover the entire surface with something (either collage material or a precoat); otherwise it will get stuck in your printer!

FIGURE 19.11 Smooth the foil down as flat as you can with a brayer.

FIGURE 19.12 Burnish down the foil as much as possible.

FIGURE 19.13 Apply a complete, even layer of precoat to your surface.

4. Press the foil down by hand, and then use a brayer to smooth it down (**Figure 19.11**).

5. Wrap a piece of foam insulation in a plastic bag, and then burnish down the foil (**Figure 19.12**).

6. Use a spreading bar or sponge brush and apply your inkjet precoat over the entire surface. The precoat will seal in both the aluminum and acrylic emulsion. Allow it to dry completely (**Figure 19.13**).

7. This is a good time to smash the sheet well with a large brayer, steel roller, or laminator. Pass it through your slot ruler (see Chapter 17), and pound down any areas that are too high.

8. Run your hand over your substrate. If you can feel the acrylic emulsion (it'll still be sticky), apply a second layer of inkjet precoat and allow it to dry completely. Repeat until the surface no longer feels sticky.

9. Take a photograph of your completed substrate, and then follow the instructions in Chapter 3 to digitally combine it with a substrate and create your image file for this project. Make sure your image is ½" larger than the substrate.

10. Cut a piece of Pellon fabric at least 3 inches longer than your substrate (you can stick two pieces together with tape, if necessary). Then use strong double-sided tape on all the edges of the substrate and mount the substrate on the fabric—leave a 3" lead of plain fabric to feed into the printer. Run this through your slot ruler one more time to make sure it's still thin enough (**Figure 19.14**).

11. Set the platen gap to the widest setting, and set the print options on your computer to start printing 2.5" from the lower right edge. Because the image is larger than the foil collage, it will bleed off the edges. Verify all your settings, and then print your image (**Figure 19.15**).

12. Depending on which precoat you used, the ink may be tacky for several days. In any case, no matter how dry it feels, allow the panel to sit for three to seven days before applying a postcoat and before framing it. Pigment inks have a solvent that needs to gas out before you seal the surface.

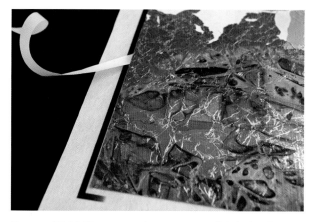

FIGURE 19.14 Tape your substrate to your fabric, leaving a 3" leader.

FIGURE 19.15 It's always exciting to see how the image and substrate combine.

FIGURE 19.16 The title of this 32" x 40" direct print onto aluminum foil is *Blue Ice*.

Conclusion

These two processes build on the basic direct printing technique in Chapter 18. The more complex substrates and the additional carrier sheet method bring a rich variety of additional creative choices to your studio. In the next chapter, we'll build on these even more, and push the limits of what this technology can do.

20

DIRECT PRINTING onto Custom Substrates

N ow you have another chance to get out the paints and get away from the computer for a while. I love using real paint because it frees me up to play, letting the paint dictate the image instead of starting with a photograph from my digital camera. If you've never used paints and want to give it a try, go for it! It'll help you learn to think differently about what makes an image—fiber texture, brush strokes, and accidents all combine to expand your visual vocabulary. If you'd rather print a photograph onto one of these cool substrates without any special underpainting, that's fine too—it's your artistic vision!

For this first of two processes, we'll create a look similar to a gesso-coated canvas, and for the second, a paint skin that can be removed and applied to a canvas or cut apart and used as a paint skin collage.

Please read through all of the instructions before beginning the procedures in this chapter so that you have the items you need already prepared.

About Direct Printing onto a Custom Substrate

As I've mentioned various times in the book, you can either start with a custom substrate and then make your digital image, or start with your image and then make your substrate. This chapter will illustrate both processes. Each will use a carrier sheet (see Chapter 2) to support the hand-made substrate. For the first process, we'll actually use two carrier sheets—one for assembly (a polypropylene slab), and a second one for imaging (a sheet of spunbonded polyester).

HINT: I use Liquitex Gesso because it dries with a matte finish and is less sticky than other brands.

HINT: The slab should be the size that you want to print your image. However, it has to be at least six inches narrower than your printer's width if you're using a wide format printer, or two inches narrower than your printer's width if you're using a desktop printer.

MATERIALS NEEDED

- ⚠ ½" thick slab of polypropylene
- ⚠ Golden Polymer Medium (gloss)
- ⚠ Liquitex Gesso
- ⚠ Tarlatan fabric
- ⚠ Golden Black Gesso
- ⚠ Inkjet precoat (I use rabbit skin glue in this example)
- ⚠ Plain paper the same size as your slab
- ⚠ Cardboard tube as wide as your slab
- ⚠ Sheet of spunbonded polyester, as wide as your printer and at least 7" longer than your slab

TOOLS NEEDED

- ⚠ Safety equipment
- ⚠ Hard, smooth work surface
- ⚠ Sponge paint rollers
- ⚠ Brush
- ⚠ Paint pad
- ⚠ Sharp razor
- ⚠ Double-sided tape

To direct print onto a tarlatan custom canvas:

1. Use a sponge roller to apply an evenly thick coat of polymer medium (gloss) to your polypropylene slab. This creates a release layer. Once it's dry, use your roller to apply a coating of gesso (**Figure 20.1**).

2. Before the gesso dries, place a layer of tarlatan fabric on the slab, add more gesso, and then smooth out the fabric (**Figure 20.2**).

3. Place a second layer of tarlatan on the slab, apply more gesso, and smooth out any new wrinkles. Allow the sheet to dry completely. The coarse grain of the tarlatan adds a nice texture to the final image (**Figure 20.3**).

4. Once the slab is dry, apply a thick layer of black gesso to the surface of the tarlatan. Work the black into the grain of the fabric, but don't leave globs on the surface (**Figure 20.4**). Set this substrate aside and allow it to dry completely.

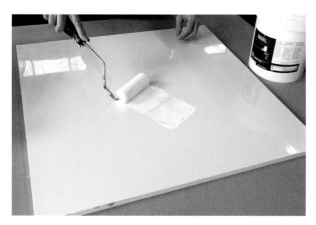

FIGURE 20.1 Spread an even coat of gesso on your panel.

FIGURE 20.2 Layer the tarlatan fabric on the slab, and then paint on more gesso.

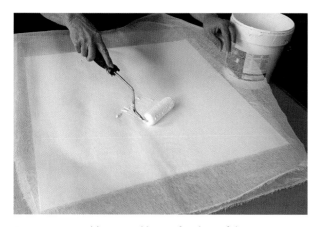

FIGURE 20.3 Add a second layer of tarlatan fabric to your slab, and more gesso.

FIGURE 20.4 Roll on black gesso, making sure you cover the entire surface of the slab.

FIGURE 20.5 Use a stiff brush to paint white onto your surface.

FIGURE 20.6 Rabbit skin glue ready to be prepared and applied to the painted substrate.

FIGURE 20.7 Save ink by printing your template without the center portion of the image.

5. After the substrate is dry a second time, apply white paint across the surface. Only the areas that are white will show the printed image, so this is your chance to create a really interesting textured surface (**Figure 20.5**).

> *HINT:* *To get loose and open brush strokes, you can create a special brush. Dip a new bristle brush into polymer medium, wipe out the excess medium and spread the bristles. Allow the brush to dry. This altered stiff brush can now be used to give a different texture to your surface.*

6. Let the substrate dry completely for a couple of days, and then apply an inkjet precoat according to the steps in the sidebar on the next page. For this example, I've used rabbit skin glue and, while still warm, spread it onto the surface with a paint pad (**Figure 20.6**).

7. Prepare your digital image by setting it to be one half to one inch larger than your substrate. Save it, and then make a separate copy. You will use this copy to make a template carrier sheet. In that copy, cut out the center of the image (to save ink) so that a one inch border of the image remains.

8. Set the platen gap appropriately, and then load a sheet of spunbonded polyester into your printer. If you're using a desktop printer, set it to print offset from the bottom by three inches. If you're using a wide format printer, set it to print offset from both the bottom and sides by three inches.

9. Print the prepared digital image from Step 7 (the one that is only the border) onto the polyester sheet. This is your template carrier sheet. (**Figure 20.7**).

PREPARING RABBIT SKIN GLUE AS AN INKJET PRECOAT

This is one of the original inkjet precoats, and I still use it with some of my work. The precoat is required so that inkjet inks don't bleed or soak into the surface of your substrate. A print on rabbit skin glue precoat doesn't dry as fast as the Universal precoat but it's cheaper, readily available, and works for many processes. Just make sure you give the print plenty of time to dry.

1. Place 1 tablespoon of the glue granules in ½ cup of cold water, and allow to swell for several hours.

2. Warm the mixture between to 130 and 140 degrees in either a double boiler or microwave.

3. Let the mixture cool to around 80 degrees, and then use a paint pad to spread the liquid onto your substrate. Make sure you don't brush over areas once they've started to gel or you'll scrape off your precoat. You should also discard any unused glue.

4. Let the coated substrate dry for at least a day, and then use a sharp razor to cut the material right at the edge of the slab. Start at one edge and separate the material from the slab. Place a sheet of paper on the slab, and then place the substrate face down on the paper. Roll the substrate and paper onto a cardboard tube. Store the substrate on the tube until ready to use (**Figure** 20.8).

FIGURE 20.8 Roll your substrate onto a tube between a piece of paper.

10. Unroll your substrate and place it face down on the table. Apply double-sided tape to all four edges. Make sure you include the corners (**Figure 20.9**).

11. Flip your substrate right side up and position it in the center of the printed template. Press down the taped edges, and run the substrate through your slot ruler to be safe. Also, feel the edges for any loose threads and trim them off with your razor. Don't skip these steps, or you risk damaging your printer (**Figure 20.10**)!

12. Set your platen gap properly again, and print your image using the same settings as before (**Figure 20.11**).

13. Depending on which precoat you used, the ink may be tacky for several days. No matter how dry it feels, allow the panel to sit for three to seven days before applying a postcoat and before framing it. Pigment inks have a solvent that needs to gas out before you seal the surface.

HINT: As a general precaution, you should not use rabbit skin glue in any printer with pizza wheels. Because the glue stays wet longer, when you go to print on your substrate, the pizza wheels could leave marks on the image as it exits. This is especially a problem in a damp climate with high humidity.

FIGURE 20.9 Tape all four edges of the substrate, and then remove the paper backing.

FIGURE 20.10 Center your substrate in the printed template.

FIGURE 20.11 Printing onto a custom substrate is a little like Christmas—you never know what it'll look like until it arrives!

FIGURE 20.12 The title of this 24" x 24" direct print onto tarlatan is *Old Phone*.

VARIATION:

Direct Printing onto a Paint Skin

This is one of the most unique processes in the book. Starting with a carrier sheet, you'll add polymer medium as a base skin, then create an underpainting of your choice, followed by more coatings of polymer medium, and then an inkjet precoat. Finally, you will direct print your digital image onto the paint skin resulting in a *paint skin* print. You can either apply this print to canvas or use it as paint skin collage materials in mixed media work.

MATERIALS NEEDED

⚠ Golden Polymer Medium (gloss)

⚠ Inkjet precoat (this example uses DASS Universal Precoat)

⚠ Polypropylene, ultra-thin carrier sheet

⚠ Acrylic paints

⚠ Cardboard tube as wide as the carrier sheet

⚠ White paper as wide as the carrier sheet

TOOLS NEEDED

⚠ Safety equipment

⚠ Hard, smooth work surface

⚠ Blue painter's tape

⚠ Foam paint roller

⚠ Paint brushes

⚠ Double-sided tape

To create a direct print onto a paint skin:

1. Apply a strip of blue painter's tape to the front of your carrier sheet around all four edges. Coat the sheet with polymer medium (gloss) using a foam paint roller, making sure you paint over the blue tape (**Figure 20.13**). Allow this to dry completely, and then apply a second coat.

   These coatings of polymer medium will become the base skin for the painting that you'll peel off the carrier sheet at the end of the process.

2. You're now ready to create an underpainting for a digital image. This can be a simple textured pattern, or a complex abstract painting that will integrate with the digital file (**Figure 20.14**).

3. Allow the painting to dry completely, and then use your foam roller to apply two more overcoats of polymer medium (gloss). Allow the painting to dry between the coatings.

4. Carefully remove the blue tape, which will leave a nice clean edge on the paint skin (**Figure 20.15**).

5. Let the acrylic paint skin dry several days before proceeding with the inkjet precoat.

FIGURE 20.13 Roll on two even coatings of the medium, covering the tape.

FIGURE 20.14 Create as simple or complex an underpainting as you like.

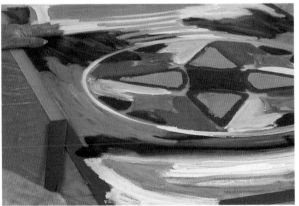

FIGURE 20.15 To cut the paint cleanly, pull sideways and away when you remove the tape.

FIGURE 20.16 Apply an even, smooth layer of precoat to your paint skin.

6. Use a coating bar or rod to apply one coating of your precoat over the entire surface. In **Figure 20.16**, I'm using a coating bar. If you're careful, you can get by with one layer as long as it soaks into the paint and completely coats the surface. You can let it dry and apply a second layer if you missed any spots, but it's better to have gotten it right the first time. Allow it to dry completely.

7. Take a photograph of your completed substrate, and then follow the instructions in Chapter 3 to digitally combine an image with a substrate and create your image file for this project. Make sure your image is the same size as your skin (**Figure 20.17**).

8. Run your carrier sheet and skin through your slot ruler to make sure they will fit into your printer, and then roll them backwards between a sheet of paper and a cardboard tube. Leave the carrier sheet and skin for 10 or 15 minutes to add a slight curl, which will help as you feed it into the printer (**Figure 20.18**).

9. Attach a 12"-long piece of white paper to the back of your carrier sheet (across the entire width) using double-sided tape. This allows the printer to see and feed the carrier sheet. If you're going to print on the entire sheet, then you'll need to add a tail to the back end as well to keep it from falling out of the printer.

10. Set the platen gap to the widest setting, and feed the paper leader into your printer. Verify all your settings, and then direct print your digital image onto your paint skin (**Figure 20.19**).

11. Allow the print to dry for three to seven days before removing it from the carrier sheet. Because the sheet is impermeable, it takes a long time to dry out completely. Removing it too soon may cause it to wrinkle or tear.

FIGURE 20.17 Left, the paint skin; Center, the digital file; Right, the digitally-combined image.

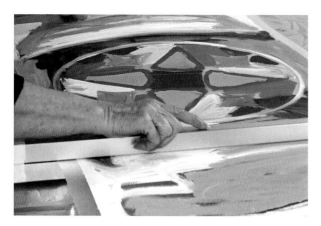

FIGURE 20.18 Always check the thickness of every substrate using your custom-made slot ruler (see Chapter 17).

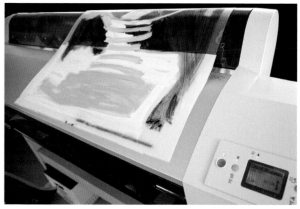

FIGURE 20.19 You can print this with a desktop printer too, as long as it can take the ultra-thin carrier sheet.

FIGURE **20.20** The title of this 24" x 40" direct print onto paint skin is *School*.

Conclusion

Approaching a new work without a plan in mind can be intimidating, yet it is an opportunity to push your own artistic limits. Embrace the unexpected as you work with the materials, and you may find that it takes your work to a new level. I enjoy these processes because it lets me play with real paint again, and yet leverage the technology that's become integral to my work. The computer and digital camera are just two of many tools that can be used to create an image. If you know you're going to add traditional media or a custom substrate to those tools, you'll start to think differently about what to look for when you frame your next photograph.

21

Gallery of Work: Direct Printing

A Wish (backside)

30" x 40". Direct Print onto a Custom Substrate. I built a tissue collage on an ultra-thin carrier sheet, and then applied an inkjet precoat. After it dried, I printed the image in a wide format printer and removed the print from the carrier sheet. After gluing it to a $3/16$"-thick sheet of polycarbonate with polymer medium (gloss), I allowed it to dry and then added acrylic paint to parts of the image, as you can see in this view of the reverse side.

A Wish (front side)

30" x 40". Direct Print onto a Custom Substrate. I display the work from this side, which is the glass-smooth surface. The thick polycarbonate removes and isolates the view in the same way that a window separates you from the outside world.

Baby Skin

22" x 30". Direct Print onto a Custom Substrate. I assembled a tissue collage on a carrier sheet and then printed it on a wide format printer. Before applying the precoat, I applied extra layers of polymer medium (gloss), which made the sheet very transparent. Then I mounted the top of the tissue skin to a rag board so it floats inside a shadow box.

Service Man

24" x 24". Direct Print onto a Custom Substrate. I used a spunbonded polyester base carrier sheet that became part of the final art. After coating it with a mixture of silica sand and titanium white paint, I used a stick to draw in the sandy surface. After that dried, I brushed off the loose sand and then applied an inkjet precoat. As always, I passed it through my slot ruler before printing.

Baby Doll

24" x 30". Direct Print onto a Custom Substrate. I mixed gesso, powdered white pigment, and athletic field marker, and then applied a thick layer to a sheet of spunbonded polyester. The coarse granules in the powder made a nice texture, while the small grains absorbed more ink, making them stand out even more.

Toys

22" x 30". Direct Print onto a Custom Substrate. I started with an old sheet of scrap aluminum that had been used for offset printing. After pounding down the corners and washing it thoroughly, I applied white paint and an inkjet precoat. My slot ruler confirmed that it would fit easily in my printer. After printing, I decided to leave the clip holes as part of the final work.

Blue Moon

24" x 30". Direct Print onto a Custom Substrate. I made a collage of silk thread and paint on a sheet of polycarbonate, using polymer medium (gloss) as a glue so that the sheet would remain transparent. The printed image of the blue leaves and seedpods remains transparent. After it dried, I placed it over a background that was painted with pearlescent acrylic paint to create a soft glow throughout the image.

Canal

24" x 24". Direct Print onto Metal. I used a sheet of aluminum roof flashing and then sanded, washed, and coated the gold side of the metal before printing it using the template method. I like the full bleed effect of this process, as I can float the final work in a frame without a mat.

Field Relic

24" x 36". Direct Print onto Plastic. After sanding a sheet of thin, white acrylic to randomly damage the surface, I cleaned it and applied a precoat. This translucent sheet makes the image look a bit like wax, so to preserve that appearance I sealed it with a matte finish coating rather than a glossy one.

Hill Top

20" x 30". Direct Print onto Metal. Sometimes, keeping things simple adds the most to a photograph. I started with the gray side of an old offset printing plate, then applied white paint and used a comb to rake through the paint to create a pattern that looks like grass. This is an example of how you can add texture to your photograph from your substrate. These hand-created works are sold as originals, not editions.

Patty Wagon

8" x 10". Direct Print onto a Custom Substrate. Ever think about printing on a sheet of open-mesh black sandpaper? If you do, just make sure you use a backer so you don't get ink all over the inside of your printer. In this case, I thought that this unusual substrate fit the old photo very well. I first painted the screen white, painted over it with diluted gold paint, and then left the black border of the screen unpainted. The photo was from an old roll of film I bought at a flea market.

Tulip

24" x 24". Direct Print onto Yupo Paper. I created this print with an experimental InkJet precoat that I'm developing. I applied the precoat to Yupo synthetic paper. After I printed the image, the ink crackled as it dried. There is no control over the pattern of the cracking so each image is wonderfully unique.

FINISHING UP AND LOOKING AHEAD

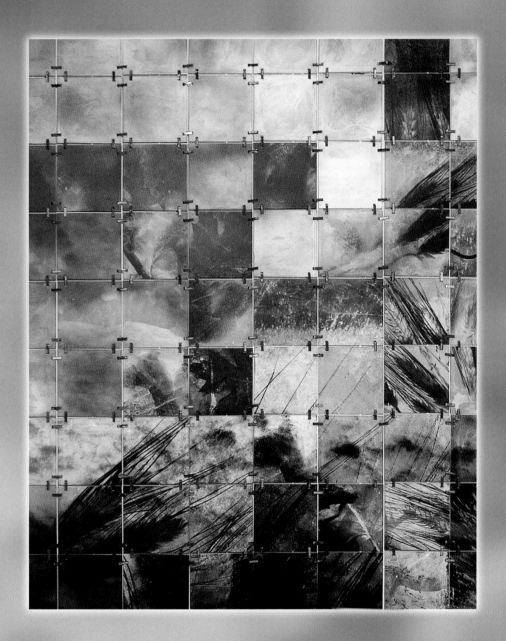

22

POSTCOATS AND FINISHING

could have called this chapter preservation and marketing, but that sounds like something out of national politics. What we're really talking about are the postcoats used to preserve your art and the finishing process that prepares your work for presentation.

Protecting all those rich colors that come out of your printer requires special techniques and there are many options you can choose from for this preservation process.

How you finish your work for final presentation is almost as important as the work itself. Putting an "old master" style frame on an abstract painting is definitely a statement...but does it work? Would you free float a Rembrandt unframed on a wall? Think about what you're trying to say not just with the art, but also with the presentation.

Read on and let me guide you through these final steps.

Postcoats

To protect your image for a lifetime of enjoyment, there are several kinds of postcoats from which you can choose. Each has specific benefits depending on the artwork itself and the artwork's intended display.

Aqueous inkjet prints need to have a protective coating applied because the inks are water soluble (as are most of the precoats). Framing in glass can mitigate this need, but if someone decides to get aggressive with their glass cleaner, you might wish you'd applied a postcoat.

UV light is another area of concern; it's the enemy of all artwork, and digital prints are no exception. Fortunately, many postcoats have a UV protectant that can reduce the effects and protect against fading.

Timing in applying a postcoat is also important. Remember to give your prints plenty of time to dry. If you apply a postcoat too quickly, the inks may fog over time. If you immediately frame a fresh print, the glass itself will eventually fog due to the out gassing of the inks. One nice thing about the transfer process is that you can print the film in advance (even months if you're using the DASS film), which allows all the gasses to escape. Then all you have to do is wait for the substrate to dry completely before mounting.

Let's take a look at the various types of postcoats and become familiar with their advantages and disadvantages.

FIGURE 22.1 Encaustic wax as your postcoat imparts a warmth to your work.

Wax

Encaustic wax is a beeswax that's prepared with a varnish. After it's melted, it's applied when still hot to the surface of a substrate. It can add visual depth to an inkjet print, but can only be used on rigid, absorbent surfaces. When used over a fresco, it imparts a rich warmth to the image. The mellow satin finish protects the inks from contaminants and moisture, but does not protect the image against UV light (**Figure 22.1**).

I prefer a very smooth finish, so I use the hot Colorado sun as a studio tool. After applying the liquid wax, I let it harden inside. Then I take the panel outside and let the direct sunlight melt the wax again (you could use heat lamps on a cold winter day). The wax flows flat in the sun, and then I carry it back inside and let it cool on a level surface. After a couple of days, I buff it with a lint-free cloth until the surface is smooth and sealed.

HINT: You might have guessed that this postcoat can melt again. In normal situations you'll be fine, but be careful about leaving such artwork in a hot car on a summer day.

Gamblin Cold Wax Medium is a nice substitute if you don't want to melt wax, but it's not quite as smooth as encaustic wax. Just spread on a thin layer, allow it to dry, and then buff it with a lint-free cloth. You can also use Johnson's Paste Wax, which is quick and easy.

The wood panel projects from Section 2 can be sealed with any of these waxes. You can even use the encaustic wax as an adhesive to build layers of printed collage paper images on birch panels (but that's another book).

Aerosol Sprays

There are two sprays that I use for my postcoats, both of which have UV protectants included in them. Krylon makes the most widely used spray varnishes for artwork. The crystal clear, non-yellowing spray is available in gloss, satin, and matte finishes. I find that it works the best to first apply a coat of gloss to seal the surface, and then apply the satin or matte as a second coat (**Figure 22.2**).

Preserve Your Memories II is a wonderful product that I use often, but it's only available in a gloss finish. You can get it as a pump non-aerosol or a paintable liquid, which gives you some nice options when working with more complex surfaces. The coating is perfect for the tile project in Chapter 13 because it creates a water-proof surface—though you still can't install the tiles in your shower (**Figure 22.3**).

FIGURE 22.2 Krylon Crystal Clear and Preserve Your Memories II are excellent postcoats.

FIGURE 22.3 Don't try this test without using Preserve Your Memories II!

FIGURE 22.4 Carefully apply water-based topcoats so that you don't move your ink.

These sprays are a good choice for any print or transfer surface, and work especially well on metal and plastic. Just make sure that your print is completely dry before applying.

Acrylic Gels

Golden Artist Colors makes a special set of Digital Ground topcoats. These are very light and spread like warm butter. This means you can apply them without the brush touching the image itself. They are water based, so if you're too aggressive, they can move the printed ink. Just go slow, use a soft touch, and be careful. They have additional UV protectants in them, and can even be used to create a brushed texture over a final image (**Figure 22.4**).

Another option is to use an acrylic or polymer medium (matte) or a gel. These can be spread on the surface of all prints, regardless of the substrate. They're flexible and won't crack. Just spread them on in thin layers, and when the work is dry, it'll appear much like the encaustic wax but without the problem of melting in heat. The one problem to note is that if the coating is too thick, your image may get cloudy in humid weather. Keep in mind that most brands don't include a UV protectant (**Figure 22.5**).

HINT: I don't like to use a gloss varnish as a postcoat because it looks too much like plastic, but you can try it if you'd like.

FIGURE 22.5 Acrylic or polymer medium is a good alternative to encaustic wax.

FIGURE 22.6 You can use a gelatin glaze as a postcoat.

A nice, simple high-gloss, smooth sealer can be made out of gelatin (see this post-coat process on the enclosed DVD). Prepare gelatin as described in Chapter 10, but change the recipe to 1 cup of water and 2½ teaspoons of gelatin. After heating, mix in ¼ cup of Golden Self-Leveling Clear Gel. Pour this fluid mixture over your panel and allow it to dry completely. This works well on a birch panel, or with the other gelatin processes, but it doesn't have a UV protectant (**Figure 22.6**).

HINT: Don't try to use the matte version of this gel because the matting agent will precipitate out in the gelatin and make the surface grainy.

Last, if you've created a work by printing on polycarbonate or other plastic substrates that remain part of the work, you can use a two-part epoxy resin as a postcoat. This cures to a very high-gloss surface, and encapsulates the entire piece. When dry, you can rub the surface with fine steel wool to achieve a semi-gloss surface. This works really well when I'm assembling larger works from a series of small tiles. While I've used this a few times and love the look, I've decided that the health risks (and having to remove my contact lenses) aren't worth doing it myself. Now I have a plastic fabricator shop coat my sheets for me—they have all the right equipment to do the process safely. Check with your local shop to see if they offer an epoxy resin with a UV protectant.

CAUTION: Make sure you read and follow all the safety information on the label if you use this epoxy resin yourself. Those warnings drove me to use an outside service to do this process, and that's what I recommend you do as well.

Liquid Laminates

There are a large variety of products in this category, so I'm only going to talk about a few. One of the best is Golden MSA varnish. It's a self-leveling product that is removable when applied to a nonporous surface. With a built-in UV protectant, it's a good choice to use on canvas or similar surfaces. The only drawback is that it's thinned using mineral spirits (make sure, as always, that you read and follow all safety precautions, as this product can be hazardous to your health). This works well over most of the paintable precoats, but if you're putting this on metal, use the Hard MSA instead.

As I noted above, Preserve Your Memories II is available as a paintable liquid post-coat. You can also use SuperSauce Solution as a varnish over any of the SuperSauce transfers in Section 2. Apply it quickly with a sponge brush, but avoid over-brushing as it will dissolve the image! This leaves the surface with a soft satin glow, and any imperfections will disappear as it dries. After a couple of weeks of drying and hardening, I apply a light coat of paste wax, which keeps moisture out of the prints when in humid climates.

Laminates

HINT: Photographs on gloss papers can be front laminated to clear acrylic sheets using an optically clear adhesive. It takes a lot of practice to do this right, so check with your local photo shop and see if they'll do it for you.

Laminates are widely used for prints on paper—most photo shops and sign shops have a laminator. The image is first mounted on metal, gator board, or another rigid backing using a double-sided laminate. Then a second over-laminate is placed across the entire surface. I see this used often in commercial applications where durable protection is needed. This technique, often called *plaque mounting*, is generally not used for fine art photographs, but I have used it for the posters for my fine art exhibits. Make sure that you pick a laminate that contains a UV protectant.

UV Acrylic Sheets

The most common way to present a photograph is framed under glass (either with or without a mat). In the early days of digital printing, UV protective acrylic was the only option available for preserving prints. Once Encad introduced protective pigment inks in 1997, the UV protective acrylic became less critical. Nevertheless, I still recommend you use UV protective acrylic sheets for works on paper rather than going back to actual glass, unless you've used a postcoat that includes a protectant. And I prefer the acrylic sheets over applying a postcoat directly to the image.

Framing and Installation

I consider the presentation of the work as part of the entire package. When I'm working on a commissioned project, I'll go visit the intended installation site and consider it in my overall design. I'll think about the location in which the piece will be hung, including such factors as room size, wall colors and coverings, other room accessories, and room lighting.

My newest presentation technique involves backlighting my work (especially when printed on a translucent substrate). I installed *Crystal Ice* in the atrium of a skyscraper here in Denver, and had custom double-slotted edge grips made. The ¼" panel goes in the front slot, and an LED light pad goes in the back. The soft illumination that this piece provides uses just four watts of power per running foot and will last for many years (**Figure 22.7**).

A similar technique is to build a light box that becomes part of the work. This is a good option if you're selling your work in a gallery and don't know how it will be displayed, or if your customer is a bit more budget minded. I use fluorescent T-8 5500K bulbs with electronic ballasts to avoid the hum that other fixtures have. I installed *The Falls* in a hospital chapel where it provides a subdued, calming centerpiece. These works still need some sort of frame, so take that into account when you're working (**Figure 22.8**).

Works made on Dibond panels have a nice edge that can be exposed and installed unframed for a very clean, contemporary look. *Eclipse* was installed in a law office using edge grip mounts. For an installation like this, the frame would have had far too much focus in the constrained space (**Figure 22.9**).

The cool thing about Dibond panels is that they're so light you can still use a frame, as with *Mystic*. Because this is hanging in a home, the work really needed a frame to set it apart from the wall (**Figure 22.10**).

FIGURE 22.7 Your substrate has to be at least ¼" thick to create a backlit, free-hanging installation like this.

FIGURE 22.8 Another way to backlight a piece is to use a light box with a white diffuser.

FIGURE 22.9 Know your installation space to help determine the best mounting approach.

FIGURE 22.10 These processes are very flexible, so you can choose from multiple mounting options.

FIGURE 22.11 I really think this unusual approach—creating a translucent border—works well in this space, and evidently so does the bank where it's hanging!

Creek was created on a sheet of ¼" sanded polycarbonate. I masked out a 1½"-wide strip on all four edges of the back side, and then painted the center area with two coats of white gesso. After it dried, I removed the tape to create a translucent border. The dark wall then created a built-in vignette around the image, which softened the transition between the installation and the work itself (**Figure 22.11**).

These transfer processes can be used to create a surround, a wide, flat wood mat as a framing device that extends the image or relates to the artwork. For *Meridian*, which is hanging in my own private collection, I had a woodworker make a flat Baltic birch frame with a 3"-wide face. You can also use raw molding from a frame shop; this is a product the shop uses to make linen-wrapped liners (**Figure 22.12**).

I'm getting tired of transporting huge crates—it costs a lot, and can be hard to find someone to carry them out of my studio. So I've started creating some of my largest works so they display like a hanging tapestry made from wood or plastic tiles. To create *Amber Wheat*, I used brass straps to hang these tiles together in my studio, and then disassembled them, packed them into smaller boxes, and reassembled them on site at a hospital (**Figure 22.13**).

FIGURE 22.12 Extend your work onto the frame itself by transferring an image to a surround.

FIGURE 22.13 There's almost no limit to how big you can make a tile tapestry.

FIGURE 22.14 Present your work on a box to make it a physical presence in the room.

Last, for the easiest of all presentations, I make the art on a series of 3"-deep boxes. This creates a work with substantial presence, and is always an unexpected surprise at an exhibition or in an installation, like this one called *Serpentine*, which is displayed in a bank. It's also cheap and easy to transport (**Figure 22.14**).

Conclusion

As artists, we have a responsibility to both our customers and our own legacy to take reasonable precautions that ensure our work lasts. In the 1990s, we didn't really know how to properly preserve digital prints. Now we do know, and even with the claimed longevity ratings for the new pigment inks, we still must take that extra step to preserve our work so that it can be enjoyed for years to come.

And when it comes to installation and display, keep the presentation stage in mind as you're creating your work. The final product is a combination of not just the materials and techniques but the presentation as well, and then—perhaps most important—your skill, talent, and artistic vision.

23

New Technology and the Future of Imaging

D aily, I run into solutions to problems I didn't know I had. At times, they present themselves as I visit reuse centers, junkyards, flea markets, or websites. I may find an item that will work for that project that's been sitting in the back of my mind for awhile, and suddenly the entire scheme solidifies into an identifiable process. Other times, I'll program my brain with a problem, have a bowl of cereal, and settle down for a good night's sleep. With my paper and pencil ready at my bedside, the solution will appear early in the morning. Something just clicks together like the glass shards in a kaleidoscope, and I get an idea for my next body of work.

I'll also go to trade shows like Southern Graphics Council (SGC), Photo Marketing Association (PMA), and the Specialty Graphic Imaging Association (SGIA) for new tools to add to my arsenal of technology. I'm fortunate to have made contacts at several high-technology and imaging companies and been involved in pushing the limits of their products to be used for fine art in ways they'd never planned.

This chapter combines a sneak peek at what's coming out of my studio, and my wish-list for what's not there yet.

UV Flatbed Printers

My number one choice for an addition to my studio is an affordable flatbed printer with white ink. Actually, I'd give up the white ink if that made it a lot more affordable (I can always use paint or a white substrate). Even with all the challenges that the current generation of these printers face, I love the way the ink builds to create the physical quality that these images have—like in *Mystic Reflection*, where I printed a photograph on Dibond brushed aluminum. This gives the work an ephemeral quality that I can't fully match in any other way. These printers also don't require the use of precoats, and you can print on nearly any material. Because of this, you can assemble a substrate (rather than collage it) from multiple materials, then print across the entire surface at once. The surface can also be much thicker and more variable than the surfaces you can print on using an inkjet printer. In the end, these UV flatbed printers are not perfect, but they're darn cool (**Figures 23.1** and **23.2**).

The closest I've come to feeling like I had one of these printers was when I spent the year traveling the country, printing on 12 different UV flatbed printers to explore the potential of the technology for use in fine art. Many of the models I used have changed, but the fundamental challenges remain the same.

At first, these machines had been criticized as being slow and for having relatively low resolution. Since I'm not producing several copies of a work at once, speed really isn't a concern (even as impatient as I get waiting to see the treasure that will

FIGURE 23.1 UV flatbed printers are a bit larger than you'd have in a home studio.

FIGURE 23.2 UV printers can create truly unique works of art, like this image of a reflected tree.

emerge). And the resolution isn't an issue because art printed on these is usually large and viewed from a distance.

One of the advantages of these printers is also a bit of an Achilles heel. They can print on really cool substrates, but the substrates are often so large and heavy that you can't use a slot ruler to check them. As a result, you may have a part of the center of the substrate that's too thick for the printer. Unfortunately, the only way to really find out for sure is to print on it. If the leading bar hits a high spot, the printer stops, which wouldn't be a problem except that most current models don't have the ability to restart and re-register the image after I've pounded down the substrate with my trusty hammer. One model I used included a laser that detected the highest spot and automatically set the head height. This would be a great feature to include on all these printers.

There are different methods these machines use to image the media. Either the media feeds under the print head or the print head moves over the substrate, and the type of substrate you have will determine which machine you can use. The first type of media feed uses grid rollers or a transport belt on the bottom. Some of these also have rubber rollers that clamp the image from the top. These really can't be used for assembled surfaces since the rubber rollers tend to catch on the uneven substrate and cause the media to feed improperly. These can print on pre-stretched canvas or thick, level substrates.

The second type of media feed uses a stationary vacuum bed, and the print head moves over the print without touching the media. This transport method makes it possible to print edge-to-edge and full bleed on very irregular assembled substrates. I love this because it also makes it possible for an artist to print an image, add additional paint or collage materials while it's still on the bed, allow it to dry, and do a final overprint on the surface. The HP Scitex Vision VEEjet uses this design, and I recently used one to print an entire tile tapestry in a single pass. I first printed a grid directly on the bed, and then laid the tiles down and sent the image to print. Amazingly easy! With these true flatbed printers, re-registering the substrate to exactly the same position when printing on both sides of clear media is very easy (**Figure 23.3**).

FIGURE 23.3 It's much easier to print tile tapestries on UV printers than one at a time on a small printer.

FIGURE 23.4 Antiqued copper cloth is easy to image when you have white ink.

With either of these types of printers, it's critical to accurately set the print head clearance. This is so important that the print operator does it with a caliper to get the right setting. Because of the tight tolerances, most print shops will not allow you to print on assembled irregular media. It's important to remember that the thickness of the media is totally independent of the distance between the substrate and the nozzles. The head still needs to be close to the surface for the image to be sharp. I found that ¼" variance in substrate surface thickness is the most that I could have to get a good image. The media itself can be several inches thick.

Of all the advantages of these printers, the addition of white ink is one of the most powerful for fine art printing. Most of these machines can print white in many different ways including underprint, overprint, spot, under-spot, and fill. Access to this capability allows me to add a white image to fine copper cloth that's been stretched on a frame, creating something that simply isn't possible in other new media technologies (**Figure 23.4**).

So how do you get white information out of a digital file that only has red, green, and blue (or cyan, magenta, yellow, and black)? In Photoshop, white is printed using a fifth channel, and then processed by the rip. A good rip with some printers can also automatically place white in areas where the image has no color.

Some machines also have the ability to use spot varnish, which adds depths to blacks and can be used to create gloss finish in selected areas of a matte image.

RIPS

A rip is a piece of software that sits between Photoshop and the printer. This software provides controls beyond what's available in Photoshop or your operating system, and is essential for printing on nearly all UV flatbed printers.

FIGURE 23.5 Clean the substrate with alcohol before printing.

FIGURE 23.6 I printed part of the image on the back side first to add depth.

This level of control greatly expands the possibilities available to the modern artist. On printers with stationary beds, I print multiple passes and vary the density to build up the image with visibly thicker and thinner areas of ink. This is especially useful for back-lit applications or for printing a 3D lenticular image directly on the lens.

As of this writing, the Fuji Acuity and Océ flatbeds with white ink are among the best machines for fine art use because they have stationary beds. These are the flatbed printers I currently use for my work. They have beds that hold the substrate down with a vacuum, which helps keep the substrate stationary between passes (**Figure 23.5**).

To use this kind of flatbed, I split the image into layers in Photoshop and use masks and gradient channels to place white under portions of the image. I print the back of the substrate first, turn it over, register it, and then print the front side of the final work (**Figures 23.6** and **23.7**).

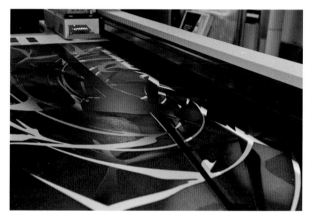

FIGURE 23.7 I then printed more parts of the image on the front.

FIGURE 23.8 This 48" x 84" piece, printed with multiple passes on a UV flatbed printer, is titled *Night Light*. It is backlit with a ¼ inch thick light pad.

For *Night Light*, shown on the previous page, I used nine different files with white layers of varying transparency. I used a double layer of white under the black turbine so that it's in silhouette when backlit. When installed, a work like this becomes a glowing presence in the room (**Figure 23.8**).

So where do you find one of these amazing machines to print on? Many sign shops now have them, but finding a shop that's willing to meet the demands of the artist is rare. Finding a shop that will let you print on assemblages is almost impossible (I did most of my flatbed research at the printer manufacturers). I have a shop that will let me buy a day at a time so that I can work with the printer at my own pace. If you're interested in trying out this technology, I suggest finding a group of artists and share the cost of a day to learn how to prepare substrates. As alternatives, I suggest trying out the processes in Sections 2 and 4—I developed these processes while working on a UV printer as I looked for a solution for proofing on my inkjet printers. They come close to the same look, at a fraction of the cost.

Check the book's website at www.digitalalchemybook.com for any updates as I continue to experiment. It's important to remember, though, that none of these printers can compete with the Epson and HP aqueous inkjet printers when it comes to resolution or color reproduction. I use the UV printers for much of my commissioned work, but when I need absolutely tack-sharp resolution and color accuracy, I still turn to my Z3200.

The other pitfall that the inkjet folks have already solved, but the UV teams need to address, is ink longevity. As of this writing (late 2010), I have not seen any longevity tests. I expect it's OK because the inks are pigments, but watch the book's website for updates as information becomes available. So far, all of my prints from 2002 show no signs of fading after hanging unprotected in a south window for eight years, which is a very good sign.

As the technology becomes more widespread and these machines grow more affordable, they are likely to become fixtures in studios, artists' co-ops, and university printmaking departments. The physical quality of the UV-cured ink and the ability to print on any surface (no more precoats!) opens amazing new possibilities for art. Art is already being produced on these, and it's only going to get better.

FIGURE 23.9 I used SuperSauce to transfer the image to the box.

FIGURE 23.10 The unmodified image transfers dried for two days.

Laser engravers

I've recently had the opportunity to experiment with the CO_2 VersaLASER from Universal Laser Systems. This is a really cool tool—you actually print your image as an engraving to the laser. I just prepare an image in Photoshop, convert it to bitmap grayscale, and press the Print button. The laser printer driver does the rest. You can also use a vector image from Adobe Illustrator to cut shapes. The printer driver has a library of materials to choose from as your substrate, including paper, wood, leather, granite, plastic, marble, glass, and metal.

A traditional printmaker could use the laser to engrave woodcuts, collograph, or etching plates. The level of control in the system is amazing, and has allowed me to develop a process to layer paint and transfers on a birch box, then burn away portions to create works I never thought possible. This is right on the cutting edge (no pun intended) of my work, so you can see more images in Chapter 24, or keep checking my own website (www.lhotka.com) as I continue to explore the technology.

I first paint the boxes white, and allow them to dry. Then I use the SuperSauce transfer to wood (see Chapter 7) to apply an image to the box (**Figure 23.9**). **Figure 23.10** shows the images drying in their full, unengraved color.

Next, I painted layers of white, pearl, bronze, black, and ivory paint on the surface, and allowed them to dry for a week. Finally, I printed the image with the laser. The amazing control over speed and intensity lets me choose exactly what paint layer will be visible (**Figure 23.11**).

FIGURE 23.11 The title of this 32" x 32" laser-engraved image is *Bone*.

3D Imaging

The consumer electronics industry is abuzz with the excitement over 3D imaging. Hollywood has fallen in love with 3D all over again (I still remember the B-rated sci-fi movies in the 1950s). Home TVs are already available that can project 3D movies, and there are now 3D cameras available at affordable prices.

3D in art has recently been monopolized by the lenticular technology. In 1999, Microlens introduced a lens and Flipsigns developed the software that allowed the creation of lenticular images on an inkjet printer. You probably know lenticular technology as the moving images in the surprise inside a box of Cracker Jacks and baseball cards. Once I found a way to do that myself, I was hooked.

Lenticular images are a unique way to create an environment in a public space, and captivate a wide audience of viewers. I have an installation in the lobby of a hospital that actually changes the mood of the lobby. I still get a kick when my grandson puts his hand through the projected image and giggles because he thinks it tickles. Art that touches in this way is remembered (**Figure 23.12**).

FIGURE **23.12** The title of this 144" x 72" 3D lenticular piece is *Field*.

FIGURE 23.13 The title of this 180" x 60" six-panel animation is *Chromatic Wave*.

Another level in 3D imaging is to create an animated image that allows the viewer to move and become involved with the piece. Because these animations require a physical lens over the image to achieve the 3D motion effect (no glasses required), you really have to see one of these in person. I made a six-panel animation with a wave that moves with you as you pass from one to another. The gradient of the color saturation from full color to near black and white also changes the mood of the art when viewed from a stationary point (**Figure 23.13**).

Another 3D imaging process is the anaglyph, a simple 3D image made from two photographs taken on the same horizontal axis about four inches apart. The red channel in the right photograph is replaced with the same channel from the left photograph. Even simpler is to purchase a Loreo lens for your digital camera. It automatically takes the pair of photos. All you need to do is swap the red channels, and view your creation with those red and green glasses we remember from school (**Figure 23.14**).

A more advanced version of the anaglyph is a phantogram, which is what I use for my artwork. These are best displayed where the viewer can be at a 45 degree angle from the work. At a recent exhibition, I displayed a series of these phantograms framed and 12 inches off the floor. The 3D effect is so powerful that the image appeared to be two feet tall (**Figure 23.15**)!

FIGURE 23.14 You can create simple 3D anaglyph images yourself.

FIGURE 23.15 These kinds of 3D images always draw a crowd.

PHANTOGRAM GLASSES

Check the resources section on the book's website for places to buy glasses to view these phantograms (and the ones in Chapter 24) in 3D. There are also links there to additional images that you can download to your iPhone.

At my openings, these phantograms always draw a huge crowd, and it's fun to watch people clustered around them, waving their hands through them, laughing like kids at the amusement park.

Conclusion

Many of the processes in this book were only developed in the past year, so one could argue that the whole thing is a look to the future of imaging. This chapter talked about processes that are beyond the cutting edge, and I'm just beginning to explore their limits. If you have a chance to try them out, by all means do so—the more artists and photographers who use them, the broader the market, and the sooner we'll all be able to have them in our studios!

FIGURE **23.16** The title of this 32" x 32" phantogram is *Water*.

24

GALLERY OF WORK:
NEW TECHNOLOGY

Carbon

48" x 48". Laser Engraving on Birch Box. I started out by painting the boxes in layers of black, white, and yellow acrylic paints. Then I converted the image file to black and white, and processed it with special image processing software from Andromeda Software, Inc. to achieve this look. I printed the image using a CO2 laser, which burned off the surface in different layers to expose the colors.

Diamond

32" x 40". Pearloid Transfer. I'm developing a new type of transfer that creates images similar to daguerreotype photographs, but without all the toxic chemicals. These are stunning in person—the images have a reflective glow under the glass surface. Stay tuned to the book's website for new developments on this process!

Spring

48" x 46". UV-Cured Pigment on Frosted Acrylic Plastic. This substrate is something I'm
starting to experiment with. For this image, I printed the white ink on the back of the ¼" sheet
of plastic, while the front holds the colored image. Any white you see on the front is due to the
sanded finish on the plastic sheet. This is a great example of the potential of UV imaging.

Organic Replication

32" x 32". UV-Cured Pigment Print. I stretched copper cloth over a frame, and then placed it face down on a plastic sheet. After adding vinegar and salt, I left it to age. Once dried, I only brushed it off, and then printed directly onto the patina. I wanted a really good postcoat, so I had the entire surface sprayed with a polymer at a local plastic coating shop. The postcoat is undetectable on the fine mesh—I expect to use this polymer postcoat for other works in the future.

Civic Center

48" x 46". UV-Cured Pigment Print. I used a UV printer (that didn't have white ink), and printed with a frosted acrylic plastic as a substrate. The twist is that I printed half the image on the front and half on the back, and then placed a full mirror behind the image to make it glow in gallery lighting.

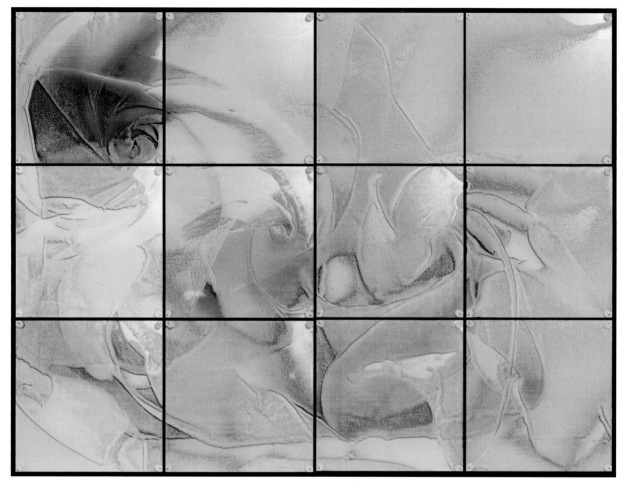

White Light

72" x 54". Multiple Processes. I started out by cutting the image of a gardenia into twelve 18" square sections. Then I used the SuperSauce to plastic transfer, placing an image on the back of each plastic panel. In the next step, I engraved the image onto the front of each panel, and then mounted it on a 3" x 18" x 18" painted birch box. I even used a laser to make acrylic washers, engraved and cut in the shape of a gardenia bud, to secure the corners of each panel. I like it so much that this one may stay in my private collection!

Wind

36" x 36". Phantogram. I started out with an HDR print of a cloud as a base to set up a still life.
The boat is a ship model built by my great uncle in the 1800s. I made the pinwheels from a
second copy of the cloud print, glued them to sticks, and then set them upright in the base. I
photographed it in HDR and then assembled the image as a phantogram.

Earth

36" x 36". Phantogram. I used an HDR photo I'd taken at the Denver Botanic Gardens as a base
for another still life. I took a second print of the image and cut out seed pods, and placed them
so they appear to be growing from the base. Then I added an antique water can, dry roses, and
silk foliage. Once again, I shot the still life as an HDR phantogram.

24K Gold

66" x 78". Laser Engraving on Birch Box. I photographed a collection of my mom's treasures, representing special memories I have of her. These are so precious that it seemed only appropriate to seal the memories in gold. I painted the set of birch boxes with layers of black and white paint, and then covered the tops in 24K gold spray paint. Finally, I printed the image using the laser, which burned away enough of the gold to create an ash-colored image beneath the surface.

Garden Gold

32" x 32". Laser Engraving on Birch Box. I used SuperSauce to transfer a very color-saturated image to the surface, and then fully covered the image with three layers of white gesso. Finally, I sprayed the boxes with gold paint, and used the laser to cut through the painted layer to reveal the transferred image beneath the surface.

Sitting Duck

24" x 24". UV Pigment Print on Plastic Over a Lenticular Image. I printed a photograph of a salt washed sea wall on one side of a plastic sheet, and later cut two holes out of it. I finished the piece by creating a 3D lenticular image from 32 photographs taken in sequence, and placing it behind the holes to create both a real and simulated 3D effect in the work.

White Fish

32" x 40". 3D Lenticular Print. I took a single photograph of a Koi pond, and mapped it across a grayscale mask to create the depth I wanted. After interlacing the 32-frame set, I printed it and laminated it to the lens. The U-shaped, mat-like surround visually projects three inches out from the surface. The fish visually recede three inches below in the center, as if you were looking down onto them from above. This is another work that's hard to capture without seeing it in person. You can check my website (www.lhotka.com) for current and upcoming exhibitions.

Index

wire brush, 29, 126, 140

A Wish, 246, 247

Wizard, 51

wood

    baltic birch boxes/panels, 17, 75, 124–125

    sawdust, 28, 77

wood substrates

    considerations, 16–17

    preparing for gelatin transfers, 124–125

    SuperSauce transfer to, 75–81

work surface, hard, smooth, 38, 122, 149

Y

Yupo paper, 224, 225, 257

Z

zinc-plated rods, 198

Zip disks, 11

MAY 0 3 2011

MAY 1 1 2011.

BASEMENT

WATCH
READ
CREATE

Meet Creative Edge.

A new resource of unlimited books, videos and tutorials for creatives from the world's leading experts.

Creative Edge is your one stop for inspiration, answers to technical questions and ways to stay at the top of your game so you can focus on what you do best—being creative.

All for only $24.99 per month for access—any day any time you need it.

peachpit.com/creativeedge